ALEXANDER CAMPBELL:
A COLLECTION
VOLUME 1

ALEXANDER CAMPBELL
ARCHIBALD MCLEAN
THOMAS CHALMERS

EDITED BY
BRADLEY S. COBB

Charleston, AR:
COBB PUBLISHING
2024

Published in the United States of America by

Cobb Publishing
704 E. Main St.
Charleston, AR 72933
www.CobbPublishing.com
CobbPublishing@gmail.com
479.747.8372.

ISBN: 979-8-3303-2077-6

Changes in this Edition

The works contained in this edition have undergone several changes. Don't worry, nothing was left out. I hope you will agree that these changes make for a more pleasant reading experience.

1. The fonts have been changed and enlarged to make for easier reading and a more modern-looking publication.

2. Spelling has been updated to conform to modern usage.

3. Obvious typos have been corrected.

4. Many quotations have been indented and set apart, conforming to modern standards.

5. *Alexander Campbell's Tour in Scotland* did not originally have chapter titles. These were added for this revised edition, using quotations from each chapter.

6. Because of the corrections above, and the nature of this book, the page numbers here will differ from the original.

Contents

Delusions: An Analysis of the Book of Mormon 116

Demonology 146

ALEXANDER CAMPBELL'S TOUR IN SCOTLAND

By Thomas Chalmers

A. CAMPBELL.

Anno Ætat 65

Preface

In justice to myself and respect to the reader, it is but right that I state here, that when the papers of this little book began to appear in **THE GUIDE**, it was no thought of mine that they should ever take a more permanent form; and it has been only at the urgent desire of many friends, known and unknown, that I consented to their publication. During the four months while these papers were being written and published weekly, the author was busier than at any other time in his life. With the care of a congregation of over five hundred members, the editing of a bi-weekly church paper, preaching every night for three weeks of that time, moving from one congregation to another with all the burdens and confusion incident to such a change, doing considerable other miscellaneous writing, he wrote these papers, each one as it was needed by the publisher.

The narrative as a whole is authentic, though it would be too much for me to claim that I have produced *verbatim* the speeches of my informants. The whole matter required such a developing as to make it symmetrical and complete, and this I have not hesitated to do, though it has been my constant aim to be true to my text.

If the story here told leads the young people of our homes, our Sunday-schools, and our societies of Christian endeavor, to a better appreciation and a greater interest in one of America's chief reformers, it will have fulfilled its mission.

THOMAS CHALMERS.

Brooklyn, N. Y., March *25, 1892.*

Introduction

Alexander Campbell appeared on the field of religious conflict at a "psychological moment." The disturbed condition of theology in the public mind demanded the work which he did. There was a lull in the battle which had raged on Christian territory for more than three centuries. Persecutions had ceased, the mighty engines of the Inquisition rested, and the last embers of the fagots at the stake had become cold. The lull was one of dazed confusion. The warriors had stopped to breathe and look about them to see really who was right and who was wrong. They surely could not all be right, but for toleration's sake—for peace and rest—each one decided to give all the others over to Satan and perdition, and let them work their own damnation if they chose.

That something was out of joint was plain, but in the unskilled theological surgery of the time, no one could see just where the fracture was, or how to deal with it. Just then Alexander Campbell came. "We are all wrong," said he, "and can never live in Christian concord, even though we may agree to practice mutual forbearance so long as we stand off looking at each other at these angles. Let us return to the original church as it is developed and portrayed in Scripture." That was a novel idea. The disputants looked each other in the face and smiled; but many were ashamed to obey the summons immediately, though it had a salutary effect even on those who stood still in their tracks, and from that day many have been the longing, lingering glances cast toward the primitive church. And we may be assured that, from this day on, the great Christian movements which contain the elements of permanency, will be in the direction of the early church.

The present religious awakening in France will carry the church, says M. Vogue, toward a more "primitive evangelical faith," The waves of Campbell's influence have spread far beyond the circle of his own religious household. In a conversation last year with one of the most eminent clergymen in New York City, who has been the spokesman of his denomination for Christian unity, I found what seemed to be an explanation for his progressive spirit and views when he said he had early read much of Campbell's writings. I would not, however, be understood to believe that the great movements of which I speak, are the effects of this one man's influence. They have a greater meaning for me than that— but that Alexander Campbell was the greatest and ablest exponent of the idea which underlies these movements, as Calvin was of the Divine Sovereignty idea, Wesley of the personal piety idea, and Channing of the divine humanity idea, is what I mean to say. His name stands for the new doctrine, of a return to the conditions of primitive Christianity. "To come firmly and fairly to original ground," taking up things where the apostles left them; to be able to produce a "Thus saith the Lord," either in expressed statement or approved precedent, for everything *that is required;* to rebuild the walls of the spiritual Jerusalem; —this is *Campbellism* if Campbellism is anything, and if any one wishes to apply to these *human* efforts that name, and is understood to mean no more, it would be difficult to reject the designation.

A sketch of Campbell's life and the external or objective conditions that contributed to the success of his great ecclesiastical enterprise viewed in relation to his great intellectual make-up, should be the trend of these preliminary pages.

Alexander Campbell was born in Antrim County, Ireland, September 12, 1788. His maternal ancestors were Huguenots who, driven from France, after Louis XIV had revoked the edict of Nantes, had sought refuge among the Presbyterian population of the North of Ireland. The blood of these intelligent, God-fearing, but man-defying and courageous Frenchmen was no slight legacy. On his father's side Alexander was of Highland Scotch descent. No Highland clan has played more important and respectable a part in the history of the world than has the chin Campbell of Argyle. It was on the territory of this clan, and through its steady support that the light of Christianity and education, as kindled on the little isle of Iona by Columba, in the sixth century, was long kept burning, and it was as late as the eleventh century that the ancient and purer religion of the Culdees was replaced on the western coasts of Scotland by the ecclesiasticism of Rome. There is something innately inimical to religious corruption in the sturdy stock of the western isles of Scotland, for it was here that the restored Gospel in the early days of Protestantism was received back again, as something precious but lost, by these people who have so stoutly maintained it since. The Roman church held dominion for less than five centuries over the Scottish ancestors of Alexander Campbell. His grandfather was a Roman Catholic, but became an Episcopalian; his father, Thomas Campbell, advanced one step farther and became a Presbyterian, and Alexander completed the return to the primitive faith. These steps indicate the tendency of the stock; there was something in it antagonistic to ecclesiastical power and ritual, and whenever a step was taken, the face was turned toward Jerusalem. Opposite tendencies are often noticed. In the early part of this century the Oxford movement made itself felt in the whole religious society of England, turning the faces of Puritans toward Canterbury, and of Anglicans toward Rome where its logical end was, and resulting as it inevitably would, in a wide-spread secession to the Roman church, where Newman, Pusey, Keble and Froude constitutionally belonged any way. There was no cause of alarm to Protestants; it was a natural and temporal reaction from the uncouthness and ugliness in the Puritan idea of worship. But the faces of the Campbell family were not turned toward Rome or Canterbury—they were not seeking beauty and symbolism in church worship; they were lost in the woods and were "seeking for the old paths"—they turned their faces toward the city of the Great Pentecost, that they might find the old landmarks; then beauty of worship might be considered, but not till the true church is found.

Thomas Campbell, the father of Alexander, was graduated from Glasgow University in three departments—the college, the theological seminary and the medical school. In his college class was his eminent cousin, the poet of his own name. He returned to his native place in the north of Ireland and became employed in the double profession of preaching and teaching. He founded and became the Principal of Rich Hill Academy. It was here that Alexander received the rudiments of his education, and was prepared for college. As a youth he was not remarkable for his diligence in study, being a fond lover of nature and out-of-door exercise, though to manual labor he seems, like many other boys who afterwards became eminent, to have been averse. He was, however, both physically and mentally vigorous; his mind was "alert, comprehensive and retentive, and the vast fund of information on all subjects of history and literature, in the use of which he showed such astonishing facility in his later life, was largely accumulated in these early years. He assisted his father as a teacher in the Rich Hill Academy, at the same time ho continued his own studies, under paternal tuition, and thereby developed his wonderful faculties of assimilating, arranging and distributing facts and theories as he required them. His grasp of a subject, and quick power of discrimination made him at all times consistent with himself, for no idea was ready to be dealt out until it found a place for itself in his own system of philosophy according to the fundamental principles on which he rested. His education was already a liberal and thorough one when he entered Edinburgh University in the fall of 1808. He had started with his mother and brothers and sisters for America, but the vessel was wrecked on an island off the west coast of Scotland. It was then, that, sitting on the stump of a broken mast amid the gloom and uncertainty of his surroundings, he made a covenant with God, that if he was rescued from the misfortunes of that day the services of his life would be laid at the altar of the Lord. How well he kept that promise for sixty years, all the world knows. In Glasgow University he was instructed by some of the most eminent scholars of their time—Young, the grammarian; Jardine, the logician; and Ure, the physicist. Besides the classic atmosphere of the University which he breathed, he was thrown into intimate association with some of Glasgow's greatest preachers. The man whom, more than all others, he found congenial in religious matters was the eminent Greville Ewing, divine and lexicographer, who was at that time one of the ablest advocates of the principles of Christian faith and practice, then urged by the Haldanes. Many were the doubts and questionings of young Campbell—natural condition of mind to the young collegian when his intellect is stirred to its greatest activity, and the philosophy of his childhood is being reconstructed—but his doubts and questionings never shook his faith in the fundamentals of the Christian system; they laid hold of the external trappings of the church which surrounded and obscured the orb of "the sun of righteousness."

In the summer of 1809 he, with the remainder of the family which his father, who had come to America two years before, had left in his charge, sailed a second time for the new land across the seas, this time to reach his destination safely. He was nearly two months on the sea, landing in New York, September 29. That he was by nature something of a poet, is shown by a few lines written during the voyage, on "The Ocean." In them we see his spirit of reverence, his feeling of awe in face of the powerful and grand, and his sense of the sublime. This was the character of his religious sensibilities, —it was the grandeur, glory and majesty of God as manifested in the sublime and transcendent excellence of Jesus Christ, our prophet, priest and king, which carried him to heights of pulpit eloquence that have been seldom reached. One who has witnessed a storm at sea in the night time may sec here the picture which he so thrillingly paints: —

> *"When night comes on and darkness veils the skies;*
> *When black'ning clouds and howling storms arise:*
> *When dismal horror broods upon the deep,*

And awful terrors wake the mind from sleep,
See, from the poles, the forked lightnings fly,
And paint in solemn glares the black'ning sky;
Then from the south begin the dreadful blasts,
Hark! how they roar amidst the groaning masts:
See hemp and canvas to their force give way,
And through the air in shreds and fragments stray."

Though these lines bear the marks of the youthful pen, and are clothed in the style of the eighteenth century classicism, which was about that time in its death throes, they contain a vividness of drawing and vigor of expression that make them a credit to the young man, and they doubtless would have been received with greater favor by Francis Jeffrey and the *Edinburgh Reviewers,* than was the much berated, but triumphant *Excursion.* But the swing of the pendulum of literary taste in this century has been toward Wordsworth and his Lake School.

Thomas Campbell had already, when Alexander arrived, begun the Reformation in the wilds of Western Pennsylvania. The spirit of bigotry and sectarianism was here as exclusive as it was in the Old World, where there was so much in the traditions of the soil to preserve it. The spirit of Thomas Campbell could not but grieve at the divided and discordant condition of Christians in this new land where they certainly should have dwelt together in peace and harmony, being drawn as they were near to Nature's heart, surrounded by all that was wild and primeval. But they had brought with them the creeds which were made by men in theological conflict in a distant age and land, and which ever reopened the old sores, that in the forests of America should have been permitted to heal. To bring about a better understanding between Christians of differing orders, Thomas Campbell, with a few congenial spirits, wrote and published what has become famous as *"The Declaration and Address"* of Washington,

Pennsylvania. It was a proposal to drop the denominational distinctions, such as names, creeds, etc., and take up the Bible as the only rule of faith and practice. The statement of Sir Thomas Browne in the *Religio Medici,* concerning the church, was re-adapted to the New World, and became, "Where the *Scripture* speaks, we speak; where the *Scripture* is silent, we are silent." This is the only consistent rule for Protestants. If the religion of the Bible is the religion of Protestants, what else can we say? The consistency of this principle was at once recognized by Alexander, and he determined to devote himself without pay to its advocacy. He was a young man, fresh from college, and the resolution which he here made had the appearance of the rashness of youth, and had we lived then we should have said, "A few years will cool the young man's ardor;" but the record of nearly three-score years would have falsified our surmise, for though the young man was shortly afterward offered a position of dazzling prospect as Principal of a promising Academy in Pittsburg, at what was then an enormous salary—$1,000 a year—he declined with unshaken resolution. What the future had in store for him he did not know, but, with apostolic courage, had said, "This one thing I do," and he did it; and to the day of his death he never received one dollar for his services as a preacher of the Gospel. This precedent which I believe was not repeated, but which has left its influence on the brotherhood, has been severely criticized. It has no doubt been an injury to our religious body— we might have been more vigorous today if he had set a different example—but that is not the point we are considering; it was an act of noble self-sacrifice which has made the picture of human nature brighter in these days of Mammonism. But the disinterested resolution of the young man was afterward greatly blessed even with the goods of this world.

His first sermon was preached in a near Washington, Pennsylvania, to a congregation. This day was the real opening of his career. It not only secured for him an enviable and valuable reputation in the community, but revealed to him his own powers, and these self-revelations have often more to do with our lives than the applause of the multitudes. "After the audience was dismissed, there seemed to be but one opinion as to the qualifications of the speaker. All seemed to be forcibly struck with what they had heard. The young gazed upon the youth with wondering eyes, while the older members said one to another in subdued tones, 'Why, this is a better preacher than his father!'—a decision which in view of Thomas Campbell's reputation as a speaker was one of the highest compliments they could bestow." (See Richardson's "Memoirs of A. Campbell.")

The success of this first discourse gave him plenty to do, and during the course of the first year he preached no less than one hundred and six sermons.

On March 12, 1811, he was married to a refined and beautiful young lady named Margaret Brown, the only child of a wealthy Virginian. In the following year, on the birth of their first child, the subject of infant baptism came up for consideration in practical form. Hitherto he had regarded it as a matter only of mutual forbearance on the part of Christians, and as having nothing to do with the reformation in which he was engaged. He now determined, as his custom was with troublesome questions, to make a thorough study of the whole subject, and therefore put it beyond further peradventure. He read all the pedobaptist authorities he could find, but his mind was far from satisfied with their conclusions. He then read the Greek New Testament very carefully through, examining the etymological significance of the word *baptism,* and arrived at last at the conviction that only *the immersion of believers* was scriptural baptism. He and his wife and all his father's family were accordingly baptized in Buffalo Creek, June 12, 1812, and to the Baptist preacher who immersed him he said, "I will be baptized *into the primitive Christian faith."* He was, therefore, never a Baptist in a partisan sense, but from the time of his baptism a Christian of the apostolic order. But for convenience he became connected with the Redstone Baptist Association and remained so until the agitation following his famous sermon on the law led him to seek more congenial companionship in the Mahoning Association of Ohio. This memorable discourse was delivered in a grove on the banks of Cross Creek in the picturesque scenery of West Virginia. This *"Sermon on the Law"* created such subsequent excitement in the Baptist community that it is commonly regarded as the parting of the roads between the Baptists and Disciples. The former have, however, advanced to a point as far as this sermon. The late Dr. Jeffrey of Brooklyn, a leading Baptist, preached the same sermon once before a Baptist Association in Philadelphia and at another time to one in Warren, Rhode Island, and at both times it was received with profound attention and admiration. This was a sufficient test that, if the Baptists made that discourse the signal for breaking communion with Disciples in that day, they would not do it in this.

In 1820 Campbell accepted rather reluctantly a challenge to a debate on baptism with a Rev. John Walker, a Presbyterian preacher. It was his first experience in a character of work in which he afterward so eminently distinguished himself. The debate was held at Mt. Pleasant, Ohio, and was a most obvious triumph for Campbell. The printed discussion went through two editions and widely extended the fame and influence of the rising man who had already become quite generally known as a scholar and orator. In 1823 a second debate was held with another Presbyterian preacher, named McCalla, in Washington, Kentucky. This debate being also published, and the victory quite generally conceded to Campbell, his reputation was further extended, and he became favorably known to the Baptists in Kentucky and Tennessee. In the same year he had begun the publication of *The Christian Baptist,* a monthly religious journal, polemic in tone, but devoted to the interests of no sect, unless it was to that sect which was in the early days everywhere spoken against. The effect of this publication was electrical. It was just what many were praying for. He recognizes this want from the first. In the preface to the first edition dated July 4, 1823, he says:

"We are very certain that to such as are praying for illumination and instruction in righteousness, and not availing themselves of the means afforded in the Divine Word to obtain an answer to their prayers, our remarks on many topics will appear unjust, illiberal, and even heretical; and as there are so many praying for light, and inattentive to what God has manifested in his word, there must be a multitude to oppose the way of truth and righteousness. This was the case when God's Messiah, the mighty Redeemer of Israel appeared. Ten thousand prayers were daily offered for his appearance, ten thousand wishes expressed for his advent, ten thousand orations pronounced respecting the glory and character of his reign; and strange to tell! when he appeared, the *same* ten thousand tongues were employed in his defamation! Yea, they were praying for his coming when he stood in the midst of them, as many now are praying for light when it is in their hands."

Ideas so bold, and language so forcible, could not but greatly impress the wide-awake and inquiring mind of those days of theological shaking up. "We know from acquaintance," said he, "that there is a goodly number of sensible and intelligent persons, at this day, entirely disgusted with many things *called* religious; upon the whole it is an age of inquiry." So it was, and a magazine so bristling with striking and novel expression of old truths, almost forgotten, had its place at just that time. I continue quoting from the first preface, sentences that "went home," and do what they would, whoever read them could not get away from them. They were new, but self-evident for all that. "We have been taught that we are liable to err; we have found ourselves in many errors; we candidly acknowledge that we have changed our views on many subjects, and our views have changed our actions." It was a new idea that views should have much to do with one's actions in theology. Many continued to practice what their views could hardly correspond with, and *vice versa.* That last clause rang in their ears, *"Our views have changed our actions."* Again, in the same preface, the author states that one of the rules of his life has been "Never to hold any sentiment or proposition as more certain than the evidence on which it rests; or, in other words, that our assent to a proposition should be precisely proportioned to the evidence on which it rests. All beyond this we esteem enthusiasm— all short of it, incredulity." It would be impossible for us to describe the effect produced by so few words on the minds of those who *thought* on religious subjects. Some of his utterances were fearless, even to apparent rashness, but it was the only kind of speech that had any place in the iconoclasm in which he was engaged. He deemed it a matter of no greater consequence that the heathen should be con-verted "to the popular Christianity of these times" than that popular Christians themselves should be converted to the Christianity of the New Testament. In these papers he loved to dwell on the beauty and grandeur of the Christian religion, and to lead his readers to a nobler and loftier conception of what they had before looked at only through their respective theological spectacles. Read these sublime words of the first article in the first issue: "Christianity is the perfection of that divine philanthropy which was gradually developing itself for four thousand years. It is the bright effulgence of every divine attribute, mingling and harmonizing, as the different colors in the rainbow, in the bright shining after rain, into one complete system of perfec-tions—the perfection of glory to God in the highest heaven, the per-fection of **peace** on earth, and the perfection of **good will** among men."

We have not time to dwell longer on the contents of the *Christian Baptist,* wonderful storehouse of riches. It was enlarged and changed into a more gentle and less polemical channel after a continuance of seven years, and named the *Millennial Harbinger*. The former was a paper for its day and hour; the latter, for all time.

In 1829 the most widely known debate of Campbell's life took place in Cincinnati with the great socialist, Robert Owen of New Lanark, Scotland. The latter had been establishing his cooperative communities in various parts of the United States, but found religious principles a considerable annoyance to him. He, therefore, issued a challenge at the close of a course of lectures in New Orleans to the clergy in the United States to discuss with him in public debate the evidences of Christianity, in which he would undertake to prove "twelve fundamental propositions" which we have not space to enumerate, but which were calculated to make short work of the whole Christian religion. His challenge met with no acceptance until Alexander Campbell, alarmed at the situation, for silence on the part of the clergy would be a concession of weakness, inasmuch as Robert Owen was too eminent a man to be ignored, came forward and presented himself as the defender of the assailed religion. The debate lasted eight days; it was afterward published in Cincinnati and republished in London, and, more than any other printed discussion of the issues between Christians and infidels it has served to strengthen the Christian faith. I need not further allude to this discussion here, for considerable attention is given to it in the papers of this book.

In 1830 Alexander Campbell held a place as delegate in the most illustrious assembly which ever met in Virginia—the convention to remodel the civil constitution of the Commonwealth—and in which, as delegates, were such statesmen as James Madison and James Monroe, former Presidents, Chief-Justice Marshall and John Randolph, of Roanoke.

A few years later a second great debate was held in Cincinnati—this time with Bishop, afterwards Archbishop, Purcell on the issue between Romanism and Protestantism. The learning and ability here displayed on both sides were conspicuous. It closed with the apparent satisfaction of the friends of Purcell, and with great rejoicing on the part of the Protestants.

In 1840 Campbell founded Bethany College among the romantic hills about his own home in West Virginia. This college under his inspiration, attracted the young men of minds congenial with his own, and who revered him as the sage in whom dwelt learning and philosophy, from all parts of the Union, North and South. Here a brilliant *literati* discussed the themes of God and the universe. It was an educational enterprise of considerable magnitude for those days and in those regions, and the service that it did to the cause of the Reformation in that incipient stage, cannot be overestimated. The prime movers in the Reformation were preeminently scholars, educated in the best institutions of the old world. A more educated and brilliant trio than Thomas and Alexander Campbell and Walter Scott, a graduate of Edinburgh University, has seldom appeared in the history of religious movements, and the diversity of their talents and characteristics, with the oneness of their minds in things religious, has been a legacy to the Disciple brotherhood that should be warmly cherished. The gentleness and sweet spirit of the learned patriarch are ours, and we rob ourselves of a part of our legitimate possession when we suffer these elements to rust in disuse. The fervid, emotional temperament of Walter Scott, secret of his wonderful moving power as an orator, should also be ours if we can possess it, for it was one of the elements of our early prosperity. But the personality of the supreme mind of the trio has left its impress so deeply upon us, that none of us need be charged to cling to the memory of Alexander Campbell.

In 1843 the great debate with Rev. W. L. Rice, a Presbyterian, took place in Lexington, Kentucky, at which Hon. Henry Clay presided as Moderator. Throughout the debate the boastful manner of Mr. Rice and his readiness and ingenuity in reply and improvisation, quite deceived the less intelligent listeners, and the Presbyterians were greatly encouraged with what seemed this time to have the effect of a victory. They eagerly, purchased the copyright of the debate for $2, 000, and began to publish and distribute it, but to their great disappointment, the *printed* discussion did not have the effect they had desired, and wherever it went it made converts to Campbell's views. Presbyterianism began to decline in Lexington and throughout Kentucky from secessions to the ranks of the Disciples and Baptists, and has never been vigorous since.

No view of the Reformation Campbell inaugurated is complete without a consideration of the great Kentucky Revival under B. W. Stone, which created such a sensation in those parts as has never been equaled in this country. It was a reaction from the irreligion which the struggles with the new country had brought upon those early settlers. They had wandered away from Christ, and this great revival was the loud wail or piercing cry of the child which has thoughtlessly wandered away from the side of its mother, only to suddenly look about and realize that she is lost. It is then that the child wants her mother. She cannot be soothed with sweets, or quieted with toys; — she *wants her mother.* So with these poor people in Kentucky and Tennessee who suddenly awoke to their helplessness without Christ. Nor could they be soothed with theology and creeds; they wanted to go directly to Christ. It is thus that the work of B. W. Stone ran so parallel with that of Alexander Campbell, though the men were intellectually entirely different, and the movement of the former became absorbed in that of the latter. I quote from *"The History of the Presbyterian Church in the State of Kentucky"* by Dr. Robert Davidson, a professor at the time of its publication in 1847, in Transylvania University: "In all the affairs connected with the schism (the great Revival), the organization of the Springfield Presbytery, and the subsequent formation of societies known under the various names of New Lights, Christians, Arians, Marshallites, and Stoneites, he (Stone) was the leading spirit until they were merged in the all-embracing vortex of Campbellism in 1831."

In the summer of 1847 Campbell visited Europe, but we need not more than mention it here, for the events of this tour constitute the theme of the following papers. I must, however, beg leave to quote the letter of Henry Clay, which Campbell carried with him. It is interesting both because of its author, and the relation it bears to the subject of this book.

The Rev. Dr. A. Campbell, the bearer hereof, a citizen of the United States of America, residing in the Commonwealth of Virginia, being about to make a voyage to Europe and to travel particularly in Great Britain, Ireland and Prance, I take great satisfaction in strongly recommending him to the kind offices and friendly reception and treatment of all persons with whom he may meet and wherever he may go. Dr. Campbell is among the most eminent citizens of the United States, distinguished for his great learning and ability, for his successful devotion to the education of youth, for his piety and as the head and founder of one of the most important and respectable religious communities in the United States. Nor have his great talents been exclusively confined to the religious and literary walks in which he has principally moved; he was a distinguished member, about twenty years ago, of the convention called in the State of Virginia to remodel its civil constitution, in which, besides other eminent men, were ex-Presidents Madison and Monroe, and John Marshall, the late Chief-Justice of the United States.

Dr. Campbell, whom I have the honor to regard personally as my friend, carries with him my wishes and my prayers for his health and happiness whilst abroad, and for his safe return to his country, which justly appreciates him so highly.

H. CLAY.
ASHLAND, Kentucky,
May, 1847.

What the world will have to say of Alexander Campbell cannot now be fully foreseen, but the dawn of a brighter day for his memory is certainly appearing. Among the denominations in which a half century ago no one could do him justice, and remain, arc preachers today who dwell in pulpit lectures on his life, and, in glowing terms, give him rank among the old world reformers.[1] We are truly coming to a juster appreciation of a hero "of whom the world was not worthy."

---

[1] See sermon on "Campbell, the Disciple," by Dr. Kerr B. Tapper of Denver, Colorado, in recent issue of the *Christian Standard.*

How He is Remembered by Those Who Saw Him Then.

About forty-five years ago Alexander Campbell, then in the ripeness of his age, with a life of immense labors and wonderful fruits behind him, but yet in the vigor of his intellect left his adopted America for a tour in the old world, the purpose of which was as much to disseminate the principles, to the advocacy of which he had dedicated his life, as to recuperate his relaxing strength. This tour by some of its unfortunate circumstances has become famous to all who know anything of the life of the man. It was the writer's good fortune while in Scotland a few months ago to meet two gentlemen whose reminiscences on this subject are interesting, one an aged kirk of Scotland clergyman who has a vivid remembrance of Alexander Campbell in his visit to Scotland, who heard him speak several times and bears the picture on his mind of the great American reformer as if he had but seen him yesterday. He is familiar with every circumstance of his accusation and imprisonment, with all its causes and details. But before entering into this description of our venerable Scottish friend, let us rehearse briefly the commonest outlines of these events as we have them from our biographical sources.

When Alexander Campbell left this country, he carried with him the highest respects and honor of a great nation. He was known and esteemed by the greatest Americans of his day, and was received with distinction by the representatives of our government abroad, being the guest, while in London, of Bancroft, the historian, the minister plenipotentiary at the Court of St. James. President and founder of one of our considerable colleges, a statesman with our Madisons, Monroes, Marshalls and Randolphs, the father of what Henry Clay then termed "one of the most important and respectable religious communities in the United States," he could not but receive the respectful attention of the people of Europe. In all parts of England he was received with honor, addressing large audiences in Chester, Liverpool, London, Leicester, Manchester, Newcastle and many other important cities. He was the most interesting American of his time outside of the circle of politics, and it is wonderful how wide his fame had spread on the other side of the Atlantic. When Beecher was lecturing in England in behalf of the American Union, he was in many places but little known—even before his great Liverpool address he was advertised in the Liverpool papers as a "certain Baptist preacher from America." The great audiences that assembled to hear him, knew him chiefly as a propagandist of abolition doctrine. But not so with the subject of this sketch. In no town in England was the name of the famed "American arch-heretic" unknown. The fact that the people who held his teaching were distinguished to the world only as they wore his name bears record to the greatness of his fame. The vast multitudes that filled the largest halls to hear him were not attracted as in the case of Beecher by their interest in a peculiar political crisis or the definiteness of some theme to be discussed—Alexander Campbell had no one definite theme to which he held himself nor political theory to be advocated—but by the peculiar interest which people will always have in a man who has prescribed the thought of thousands and exposed some of what Carlyle might paradoxically call the "eternal unveracities." To such a man the English people (for they are hero-worshipers) will pay homage. And it was quite generally accepted throughout English speaking nations that some of the "eternal unveracities" had been brought to light under the pick of this great American. He had laid the ax at the root of more trees than one in the woods of ecclesiasticism and the light from above was beginning to shine in with no little discomfort to the promoters of darkness, but to the great satisfaction of many that dwelt therein. He was also well known in England as the Father of a marvelously growing and intelligent religious body in America with many adherents in Great Britain. It was, then, the personality of the man that drew his great houses.

I pause here to observe that the fame of our reformer has greatly waned since his death. He is not known so widely now as he was known fifty years ago. Houghton, Mifflin & Co., in a recent series on great American reformers have not a name on the list that stands for so much in the religious thought of this age as that of Alexander Campbell but his name is not there. Washington Gladden in a recent series of lectures on great reformers stops when he arrives at Campbell. He has Channing and others but Campbell is not there. We as a people are much to blame for this. We will preach in our pulpits on Wycliffe and Luther and Bunyan but we are cautious in the mention of one who has been of more immediate service to us than all these. Many of our own people hardly know the name of this century's greatest champion of religious truth. Lest some few should call us "Campbellite" we would suffer the name of a great man to die. He was, therefore, far better known when he was a living actor on life's stage than now. The contrary is true of Wesley and others whose lives are better and more widely known now than they were in the time of their lives, because of the loyalty of their followers. If our silence concerning the great man before us is to the single glory of the Christ it is a silence worthily intended, but the recognition and praise of virtue in men can never derogate from the honor of the perfect man— the world will be better and the picture of human nature richer for the knowledge of its truly great ones.

To return to my rambles let me state that when Alexander Campbell visited England and Scotland his fame had long preceded him— interest in him was so general that even his political opinions, on slavery, and other topics were retailed and discussed. This brings us to our narrative.

Campbell Discussed on a Train

On a bright July morning, I left St. Pancreas station, London, for Scotland. The great train with its numerous coaches stood on the track for at least thirty minutes. A tumultuous crowd is on the platform; some in outing suits are going off to the lakes for a few days or weeks, others are seeing friends away. Some are excited, nervous, rushing about, and wasting time by hurrying—now they find themselves in a wrong carriage, and now they have forgotten something. Others are coolheaded and self-possessed, they are masters of the situation, they make no mistake, they forget nothing; they find themselves in the right carriage with all their luggage with them. Among these latter, I noticed a venerable looking gentleman with long hair that came down nearly to his shoulders and white as snow; he was tall and erect, the benignant smile of an English parson upon his smooth face, I watched him as he walked to the book stall and purchased the *Religious Review of Reviews.* Then he turned and came directly toward my compartment, and as he approached I saw he wore the clerical dress, which confirmed me in my surmise that he was an English clergyman. This was Goldsmith's veritable Dr. Primrose raised from the dead again. He entered my compartment, which I had been occupying alone, and seating himself opposite me, began reading the magazine I had seen him buy. Soon the bustle and hurry on the platform subsided, our tickets were examined by the guards, and the train pulled out.

I settled myself down to reading the *Times,* and noticed nothing more until we were flying through one of the most perfectly cultivated and beautiful pieces of farming country I had ever seen.

We were approaching Bedford and, as if by a mysterious influence, my thoughts began to turn upon Sloughs of Despond, Valleys of Humiliation, Hills of Difficulty, and Delectable Mountains. It had been many years since I had last read Pilgrim's Progress, but all the scenes in the wanderings of poor Christian and the picture of Bedford jail now flashed upon my mind as I had always seen them in imagination. But here I now was in the hallowed city of great Bunyan's habitation.

There, at some distance from the railroad track, stands what remains of Bedford jail, though much unlike the "Bedford gaol" of my childhood's fancy. There, within those dreary walls was a great spirit confined—no, I will not say *confined,* for a great spirit is not to be held within walls of stone, —from those dreary walls rather a great light shone to the everlasting gratitude of many that have dwelt in darkness. It was not difficult now for my friend and me to fall into conversation—here was a matter of deep mutual interest. I was thinking of Bunyan, and I knew he was. Bunyan's imprisonment became the subject of our conversation.

He being, as I supposed, an Anglican clergyman, I was cautious as to what I said about the injustice of Bunyan's treatment by the Church of England. I was, therefore, quite surprised when he not only expressed his disapproval of the English church in this matter, but criticized it very unfavorably in many others—in matters of doctrine, worship and ecclesiastical organization, ending his remark by saying it was "but the Romish church with an English name and the English sovereign for its pope." It was now plain to my mind that he was a nonconformist. I felt more interest in him than ever, and entered with greater freedom into the discussion of matters of religion. I began such an argument against church establishments generally as I thought would just please my venerable dissenter, that, therefore, I might place myself still more in his favor and be better able to learn from him all he knew of the religious condition of Great Britain.

But I was not half through with my tirade when I saw by his countenance that my ideas were not at all tasteful to him, so closing my little speech at the first stopping place, I paused to hear the effect I had produced. Imagine then my confusion when he began an earnest, but mild argument in support of church establishments, maintaining that only by them can the strongest types of national character be produced. "Non-conformity produces no really great men," said he, "it is out of the current of national life. The great men among the dissenters, the Miltons, the Wesleys, and even the founders of your own Puritan New England were reared within the influence, and educated at the colleges of church establishments;" and so he went on. I felt myself out at sea. I at first had taken my friend for an Established church clergyman, then for a non-conformist minister, but here he is neither a churchman nor a dissenter and yet a wearer of the cloth.

What could he be? He was not a Catholic priest, for but a moment ago he criticized the Anglican church as being but little better than the Romish. We were now just pulling out of Bedford, and our conversation drifted around again to Bunyan's imprisonment.

I observed that it was a strange coincidence that since the time of the Apostles, the world's greatest preachers and reformers have, some time in their lives, suffered imprisonment for their doctrine's sake—Luther, in the castle of Wartburg (though a friendly incarceration). Bunyan, the great Baptist, spent twelve years of his life here in Bedford jail. Wesley, the founder of Methodism, in a tour through Scotland, was falsely charged and thrown into prison, and Alexander Campbell, the American Reformer, suffered a similar injustice on a similar tour. As I spoke the name of Alexander Campbell, his eyes sparkled with interest. "Alexander Campbell!" said he, "yes, one of the world's truly great ones—one of the strong men that God so seldom makes. Yes, I think I ought to know something about him in his visit to Scotland; I heard him speak there several times—I had the honor of meeting him." I saw by my friend's animated countenance that he had hit upon one of his favorite topics. My own interest was intense. Here was a man who could tell me what I could not read about one of my great heroes.

I told him how I was interested in his reminiscences and left him to his narrative. He leaned back into the corner of the carriage, and gazing for a moment out of the window, began:

"The summer of 1847 is one long for me to remember. I had just finished my education, having but the previous June completed my theological course in the University of Edinburgh. I had been settled in a wealthy and comfortable parish in a small town, a short distance from the city, with a very good living. All I could ask for was mine. Matters of theology were now of especial interest to me. I was a radical adherent to the *National Kirk of Scotland,* but like all young collegians, I was always ready to hear something new.

"Religious Scotland was much interested in the two great movements then in progress in America—the New England anti-creed rationalism and Alexander Campbell's 'anti-creed iconoclasm,' as I often heard it called. I knew little more of Campbell and his teachings than what I could learn from the religious press, and this was never satisfactory. The view of him that generally prevailed was that of a heretic to all the traditions of the church and the doctrines of the scripture, such as the divine Trinity, the Holy Spirit and many others which we orthodox Scots held as vital.

"His great debate with Robert Owen in defense of the Christian religion, however, was so able and uncompromising as to the fundamental truths of Christianity that he came to be looked upon with greater respect and even gratitude by many clergymen of all faiths. Hut it served to make many fear him the more and the news of his presence in Scotland was received with no little apprehension on the part of the most of us. A large number of intelligent people in Edinburgh regarded his religious views with favor. Several members of the Congregational and Free churches had recently gone over to the small band of his followers in Edinburgh. Many of the University students, influenced by Campbellistic views, were beginning to make dangerous investigations, and it was with considerable effort that we were able to subdue the cry for 'restoration' in our own congregations. Such questions as 'Where is your scriptural authority?' and such demands as "Give me a 'Thus saith the Lord' for that" were becoming quite troublesome, especially as they came from our parishioners whose questionings we had always felt bound to satisfy. It was a very inopportune time for this greatest living preacher of heresy, who was the author of the very notions among our people that were most threatening, to visit Scotland. I was myself, though young, conservatively orthodox and fearful of the honor and stability of the doctrines of John Knox. Our great solicitude was how we might detract the public interest in Mr. Campbell from his religious views and fasten it somewhere else, or how we might entangle him in the discussion of other and unimportant questions and such as would destroy his influence with the Scottish people. You are surprised that we ministers of the gospel should stoop to such unfairness, but such things we deemed justifiable when the very foundations of Christian orthodoxy were imperiled."

"Yes," I soliloquized, "Orthodoxy! oh orthodoxy! how many crimes have been committed in thy name!"

"One Friday evening," continued my friend, "as I sat in my study, I was surprised by a call from the Congregational preacher of the town, a man named Kennedy, with whom I had not been on the most intimate terms because of the natural hostility between our congregations. I knew that some religious trouble was brewing, but such things were so common in those days of great interest in religious questions that I thought little of it. I took no papers except religious monthly publications, and was, therefore, out of the current of events. My interest was awakened, and I waited for my fellow preacher to state his mission. He came soon to the point, as he was an abrupt man, and broke out something like this: 'Scotland is on the verge of falling into the most damnable heresy. The time-honored faith of John Knox is to be tainted by the blackest Antinomianism. Alexander Campbell has been in England for a month, and is within the borders of Scotland now. He arrives in Edinburgh tomorrow, and next week has appointments in Waterloo Rooms, and will do the best he can, with the assistance of the Prince of Darkness, to destroy our religious peace. Several of my parishioners whom I had placed most dependence upon have left us and gone over to the Campbellite. Many of your members, though you may not know it, are tainted with these doctrines. Edinburgh is more disturbed than the outlying towns, and if this man preaches for one week to the audiences in Waterloo Rooms, which will be sure to flock to see him, notwithstanding all that may be done to discourage them, there will be greater sorrow in the national kirk than she has known since the *Disruption* four years ago, and greater than she can stand at this juncture. Our duty is to devise means and work together against a common enemy. It is a fact that Mr. Campbell comes from Virginia where all are slave-holders, and it is reported that he is a defender of that institution. Now, this is the issue we must catch him on. Scotland will give no hearing to any man who will apologize for man-stealing. A committee of clergymen has been called for Monday afternoon in Edinburgh, and as you would understand best the sentiment of the students, we want you to take your place as one of this committee to determine what to do in this emergency. '

"Having said all this, he did not wait for a direct answer, but in his abrupt manner left me to myself."

"Excitement was Loud against the Great American"

We left our venerable friend just where his strange consultation with the Rev. Mr. Kennedy closed—a consultation on the best means of preventing the mischief which the great American reformer was likely to cause in the religious systems then most popular in Scotland—a consultation which brought together antagonistic teachers to fight a common enemy. This was the oft-repeated story of Scotland over again.

> *"Rival clans with one another fight,*
> *Till Norsemen boats along the coast they see;*
> *Then feuds aside are laid, they all unite*
> *To meet their enemy."*

Mr. Kennedy had held his own as an Independent minister by the side of his friend's established kirk. This he did not fear, but Campbell's doctrines from far-away America had already crossed the ocean and broken into his congregation, taking from him some of his best members. And here was Alexander Campbell himself ready to upturn all Edinburgh, and with Edinburgh all religious Scotland which took its light from that intellectual and literary center. And this at the time of a great theological ferment when the restoration of the primitive church was the spirit of the age and there was a general seeking for the old paths. Verily it was a time for apprehensions and we must not surprise ourselves that our friends across the sea, so zealous for their ancient faith, were busy at this time.

Our friend the narrator, whom, by the way, we shall call the Rev. John Laird, continued his interesting story:

"When Mr. Kennedy left my study after the consultation which I have described I devoted myself to devising some means by which the religious arisings, which I knew would follow Alexander Campbell's advent into Edinburgh, might be prevented. To prevent them would be much easier than to suppress them when they had come up. This was the important question. It did not occur to me that there might be anything which we could bring personally against Mr. Campbell which would prejudice him in the eyes of Scotchmen. I had always heard of him as an earnest and disinterested preacher of the gospel, who, though the cause of great mischief by his teachings, was yet in all his circumstances in life unassailable. I was, therefore, in considerable trouble of mind when one of my parishioners, a kind, fatherly man of unusual intelligence and much piety, came in. His name was Solomon Morton. The only fault I had in him was the very thing which now was troubling me most. He was an admirer of Campbell, had first become acquainted with him by reading the Owen debate, was a, reader through a friend of the *Millennial Harbinger* and had some other of Campbell's works in his library. He had never advocated Campbellistic principles openly, though I knew that he privately indorsed the most of them. He had not been with me long when he informed me of what I had already learned, that Alexander Campbell was to give a course of lectures on the Christian religion in Waterloo Rooms, Edinburgh, the following week, and he hoped I could attend them; that he was going to attend himself and placed great expectations on seeing and hearing a man whom he considered one of the greatest of the time. He said he could not but dissent from some of his views, but on the whole he considered his work of inestimable service to the Christian world, in presenting their religion in a new and brighter light, so that it stood out clear, distinct and rational, and in teaching the world a lesson no man had ever taught before—that the Bible was a book of definite doctrine and that it may be intelligently read. Many other things I listened to, but this was enough to fulfill my darkest apprehensions. Here was one of my own parishioners who could henceforth be counted upon as a genuine Campbellite. How many more there were in my congregation I did not know; how many there were in the churches scattered through Scotland I could not tell. When my friend continued and told me how general these doctrines were becoming in Bible-reading Scotland, my fears indeed ran high. Poor National Kirk! Another split she could not stand. From now on 1 was the sworn enemy of a man I had never seen, and who had never done me harm. So far it had not for an instant occurred to me that perhaps this man was right, that he had a case of his own. I was young and impetuous; if I had been turned his way, I would have been his loudest follower, but I had turned my face away from him and my prejudice was against him.

"My brother Morton did not stop with his high expression of Mr. Campbell's services to religion and the Bible, but mentioned many things of his practical Christianity which I had not known before. One of these was that he never accepted anything for his services, in behalf of the gospel, but being a wealthy Virginia landowner, he was able to devote the whole of his time and much of his means in support of the principles of his Reformation. Here was the point on which hung all the subsequent trouble. Campbell was a Virginian and a wealthy landowner, and therefore, without doubt, a slave-holder. This was in accord with what Kennedy had said, and it was just what we wanted. Scotland so overflowing just at this time with the most radical antislavery sentiment, would never tolerate a man who had anything to do with slavery. My friend soon left me, and I immediately wrote a note to Rev. James "Robertson who was one of the few who were to meet and talk over any way of destroying the effect of Mr. Campbell's religious notions on the people of Edinburgh, and who was president of the Anti-Slavery Society, to ascertain, if possible, whether or not Campbell was a slave-holder, or what his ideas were on the subject. Our meeting and consultation as appointed was held in Edinburgh. Reverends Robertson, Kennedy and myself and many other clergymen were present, and as care had been exercised in selecting them, we were all intent upon the same aim, to shut Alexander Campbell out of Scotland. Mr. Robertson had not yet found out anything about Campbell's position on slavery, other than that he had been an owner of slaves and had liberated them, but that he was to some extent an apologist for the institution. This information immediately disarmed some of us, and we were compelled, in the sight of fairness, to say that if this man had freed his slaves, he could not be the object of attack along that line. We, therefore, dissented from any further movement against him in this direction, unless sufficient justification could be found for it in fact. But Mr. Robertson and Mr. Kennedy were very rabid and were inclined to think that condoning an evil was as censurable as actual guilt. They attributed to him sinister motives for liberating his own slaves, and advocated instant advertisement of him as a man-stealer. But against this we still emphatically protested. At last Mr. Robertson and Mr. Kennedy, who held to this as their only rope, suggested sending a committee of three to Mr. Campbell after his arrival, and finding out what his sentiments concerning slavery were. This we all assented to as fair and right. Mr. Robertson, Mr. Kennedy and another clergyman whose name I have forgotten, were appointed as this committee.

"One evening, shortly after, I went again to Edinburgh to learn the state of things, and was met at every turn with large placards, printed in crimson letters: 'Citizens of Edinburgh! Beware! Alexander Campbell of America has been a slaveholder himself, and is yet a defender of man-stealers.'

"These immense bills were stuck up in every public place in the city. Excitement was great; groups of people were seen standing everywhere, talking about Alexander Campbell, America and slavery. The tide had been turned against him. Few were the words that any one spoke in defense of one who was so branded. Occasionally a word of disapproval of such a contemptible manner of treating a stranger, whoever he was, was expressed, but on the whole the excitement was loud against the great American."

"Very Unsavory Allusions to Mr. Campbell Himself"

The evening of August 9, 1847, was a summer night such as drew out of their homes all classes of the whole city's population. The Scotch people are especially noted as a deliberative race. Questions which we would look upon as of little interest they enter into with earnestness. But upon this occasion the excitement was especially intense and discussions unusually loud. The anti-slavery fermentation was now swollen to its largest dimension, the religious state of Scotland was ready for such a convulsion as Alexander Campbell was capable and likely to produce, and he was, with many of the best and most enlightened, immensely popular. Any more attention turned into the channel of religion would have resulted in quite, a general overflow of banks and boundaries; the same excitement turned into the anti-slavery channel would result only in a harmless social ebullition.

"I looked then," continued my venerable narrator, "upon our calumnious misrepresentations with some complacency and self-justification. But this is a night I shall not soon forget. I remember passing down the West Bow to Grassmarket, and there was a vast crowd gathered together before one of these naming placards, and I heard someone saying above the noise of the multitude that 'no horsewhipping man-stealer and slave-trafficker, whether he disguised himself in the garb of a minister or not, should be permitted to sleep one night in the city of Edinburgh.' To this I heard many loud affirmative responses. It was now that the wickedness of what we had done dawned full upon me. Here was a man, for aught I knew, might be godly and honest, abused and shamefully misrepresented—a man who deserved the highest commendation for his action in the very thing for which he was so grossly maligned and spoken against. We cried loudly for abolition, but what slaves had we ever freed? This man had no anti-slavery harangues to offer, but he, though an owner of a large plantation of them, had executed abolition in his own household—yes, more than this, he had educated his slaves and sent them forth with the legacies that are greater than simple freedom—the Christian gospel and civilized citizenship.

"I could stand it no longer, and in the impulsiveness of my younger days, I started to edge my way into the crowd, that I might tell them the whole truth, and show them where the shame and evil really lay, when whom should I see coming toward me but the Rev. James Robertson himself, who recognized me immediately, and approached me smilingly.

"'The thing is working well, isn't it,' said he.

"'Yes,' I responded, 'but I'm ashamed of the whole business, and have the strongest mind in the world to get right up here and tell all these poor deluded idiots the whole truth of the matter. '

"'Pshaw! pshaw! brother Laird, you're beside yourself. We've held ourselves within the bounds of truth. And at any rate it was necessary for us to present this thing in this way, or who knows but that this man Campbell would have torn the National Kirk and all other churches from center to circumference? '

"'If the National Kirk must live only by damning the reputations of good men by the blackest misrepresentations, then I say she should die. If she cannot live as a Christian church, embodying the principles of Christ, then she should not live at all. '

"'Tut? tut! my dear boy. You're young yet. A few years will bring you about all right. And really I have not the least doubt that Campbell is a bad man. There are many very dark stories that have reached me concerning him from America. '

"'What are some of them?' I asked.

"'Oh, well, they are various in nature, and I have not the least question of their truthfulness, for I find them in some of the most reliable American journals and in letters from different individuals.

"'Name some of those journals. Perhaps I shall find them taken at the University Library. I am seeking for the facts in this case. If Alexander Campbell is a bad man, I want to know it. If he is not, I shall take no more part in this persecution. '

"'I cannot refer you definitely to the exact names of these papers. You would not likely find them at the University. But if I am not mistaken, there is a religious paper published in Washington, which speaks of the Campbellite in very harsh terms, and makes very unsavory allusions to Mr. Campbell himself. At any rate, my dear boy, we are in God's work—saving the religious peace of Scotland and promoting the cause of human liberty. '

"'Yes, but we are using the devil's way of doing it, and sooner or later we shall have to answer for all this.'

"With these words I left him."

I pause here to advert to the consultation which the committee of three, composed of Robertson, Kennedy and a gentleman named Hunter, had with Alexander Campbell in the afternoon of this same day. You will remember that the Anti-Slavery Society, a few of whose members met on this same afternoon to take measures to destroy Campbell's influence in Scotland, deputed this committee to visit him at the earliest possible moment, to learn and publish the facts in his slavery record, and his present feelings toward the institution. This committee went immediately to Mr. Campbell, apparently to pay him their respects. Their courtesy and the lines into which they directed his conversation were designed to put him at his ease, and entrap him by the unguarded utterances that any man would be likely in such circumstances to make. They therefore so planned their questions and remarks as to encourage him into a justification of the slave traffic; but in this they failed, for he very positively condemned it, saying it had wrought untold sorrow and remained the "largest, blackest spot upon the American escutcheon." He regretted that the traffic had been ever begun, and said he had always advocated the emancipation of slaves by the owners themselves, and had set them the example by freeing his own slaves after educating them in the gospel and good citizenship.

The committee felt greatly baffled in this business. It was surely not possible to make out any case on Mr. Campbell's slavery record, nor even his present position on the question. They next drew him out on the ideas of the red radical abolitionists, who were then quite generally looked upon in this country as fanatics, and with a great deal of justice. To Mr. Campbell as well as to most other great men of his time their extreme notions were both distasteful and visionary. And looking back upon them from this advanced ground we cannot see that they really played any great part in the destruction of the institution of slavery. It would have taken a long time for the eloquence of Wendell Phillips and William Lloyd Garrison to have persuaded the Southern slaveholders to emancipate, or to have convinced the United States government that it would be an act of political wisdom to forcibly break those chains of bondage. It was a great civil crisis that compelled the emancipation of the slaves of this country, and that only after sore trouble and deep deliberation, and with many misgivings and misapprehensions.

Mr. Campbell spoke his mind freely in disapproval of the course taken by the extreme abolitionists. He thought their efforts could come to no good and were calculated to throw the nation into a civil and sectional war and perhaps destroy the nation. He deplored the interference of British societies in the American situation as causing more harm than all the good they could do. He even remarked that the relation of master and servant was not of itself sinful—that the

Scriptures did not condemn it, but even recognized it. It was, however, though lawful, not expedient nor just, and he regretted its existence for many reasons, moral, political and social.

The committee, though considerably handicapped, resolved on making their fight against the great preacher, whose influence upon the religious public of Scotland they now, after having been for an hour in his presence, so greatly feared, upon this ground, for it was this or nothing—they had no other. In a few hours therefore after this pleasant and friendly chat the city of Edinburgh was aflame with the fiery posters we have called attention to.

"May the Lord have Mercy on the Villifiers of this Good Man"

The excitement on the streets of Edinburgh did not subside for several days. It was such as was calculated to make it not only unpleasant, but to a certain degree perilous for Campbell to remain in the city. My friend informs me that he, following the advice of his friends, took advantage of the intensity of the feeling against him to go to Dundee where he filled certain appointments that had been made for him. And that the truth might be fully known, he here wrote a letter to the Edinburgh *Journal* for publication, the purpose of which was to set himself right in the eyes of the Scotch public, by making known the facts of his slavery record, and the opinions he then held on the slavery question.

The editor of the *Journal,* who was closely connected with, and in the control of the anti-Campbell committee, refused to publish the letter. Several days passed in which Campbell was speaking in Dundee and elsewhere, but Edinburgh had not yet resumed her usual quiet. Misrepresentations had been freely manufactured and floated by his enemies, and contrary to the wishes of his most solicitous friends, that he should not yet appear before an Edinburgh audience, he determined to wait no longer. He had announcements made for his next appointment in Waterloo Rooms. This is the substance of my information as I received it from my friend. I now follow him again in his narrative:

"It was with grave apprehension that I read the announcement that Campbell would fill his appointment in Waterloo Rooms for Wednesday evening. I knew something of the state of feeling against him, which I feared that he did not know himself. I almost decided to write him warning, but I knew he had his friends who would surely be as wary and as careful for his welfare as I could possibly be. I greatly admired his courage, but I questioned his wisdom. He was no doubt a great man, and possessed a wonderful power over audiences, but he would find that the Scotch people are not easily played upon by the orator's skill. His fiery eloquence (for so I had imagined it) might very well avail him in flighty and unstable America, but in Scotland it might work to his disadvantage. An orator may play upon the Irish passions and fill a mob with fire and slaughter by the inflection of a word, or the skillful manipulation of the tone of his voice, but the Scotch people are moved only by the bare recital of actual injustice or the violation of an eternal principle of right. They are of a cold metaphysical turn of mind."

I am here reminded of an incident in the life of William Hazlitt.

Once in a heated discussion with Charles Lamb's brother, the latter in a moment of anger, struck him over the eye and knocked him down. His friends immediately came to his assistance and raising him from the floor bruised and bleeding, endeavored to console him.

"Oh, I don't mind anything of that kind," he responded. "Nothing ever affects me but an abstract idea." So it is with the Scotch people. They are more inflamed at the violation of an abstract principle than they would be at a blow in the face. I am speaking hyperbolically. Slavery was a matter of principle with them, and no man who stood as slavery's champion, could win their favor.

"They had been aroused against Alexander Campbell, and more than the skill of an orator would be required to turn them. His record on slavery had, I knew, been honorable and philanthropic, but the placards and newspaper articles were, strictly speaking, founded upon truth, though, in spirit, malicious misrepresentations of it. But nothing less than a bare denial of the facts upon which these accusations rested, would satisfy a Scotch audience. Attempts at explanation and apology would only make matters worse. I feared the issue of this thing. The same day that I noticed the announcement that upon

Wednesday evening Mr. Campbell would speak in Waterloo Rooms, I saw brother Morton. He came to my study as he said to counsel with me. He always came to 'counsel' with me when he thought I deserved some reproof, or might benefit by a suggestion. His spirit was so fatherly and gentle that I was always glad to see him come. Unusual gentleness marked his countenance this time. That he was uneasy, and in trouble could be plainly seen, and the cause of it was not hard to guess. His hero, a man in whom he placed the most absolute faith, and whom he knew to be more than innocent of the malignant accusations which were brought against him, was now enduring the basest persecutions that had been heaped upon any religious teacher since the days of prelacy, and this, by his own Presbyterian Scotland. And these persecutions he had learned, were partly due to the unrighteous activity of his own pastor. Poor brother Morton! This was cause enough to him for sorrow and disappointment in human nature. But more than this was troubling him. It had been whispered around through the parish that Deacon Morton was the champion of Alexander Campbell, and since Alexander Campbell was the champion of slavery, what could brother Morton be himself, but an apologist for a wicked institution? Others who had before been favorable to Campbell and his teachings on religion, were now quiet, and brother Solomon, who had exercised more valor than discretion, was likely to be taken in hand and disciplined by the Kirk session for heresy, and perhaps deprived of his office in the deaconate, which he prided himself to have held for thirty years. It had never been his thought to leave the National Kirk, nor had it ever occurred to him that in Bible- loving Scotland he could be censured for holding doctrines which the word of God plainly taught—much less disciplined for holding such doctrines by the church which rested upon the creed that made the Bible the only rule of faith and practice for Christians. He had, nevertheless, been accused of heresy, and would likely be required to vindicate himself at the church court. But such a trial was the least of his troubles. He was more solicitous now for the welfare of the great man who was at this time the object of so many poisoned arrows."

"'Brother Laird,' said he, when he had seated himself, 'May the Lord have mercy on the villifiers of this good man, for if ever sinners should cry for mercy, they should. "Do not bear false witness against thy neighbor," said God. May he take pity on those of his professed servants who have forgotten those words of his everlasting commandment. You are young, you may be forgiven for the part you have played in this dishonorable business. The effect of this evil day will require the years of eternity to measure. '

"'Brother Morton,' said I, 'I am as indignant at the issue of this business as you can be, and in much greater sorrow for it, because my hand was in it. I am in great apprehension for Mr. Campbell in his determination to appear before an Edinburgh audience Wednesday evening. Mr. Robertson and Mr. Kennedy have turned public opinion wholly their way, and Mr. Campbell will not be given a candid hearing even if the motley crowd that is likely to assemble there for mischief or curiosity should not attempt to do him injury. The whole tone of the placards and the newspaper notices is that Mr. Campbell is not a fit man to rest in the city of Edinburgh, much less presume to instruct the people on religion in a public auditorium. These are the foundations of my fears. '

"The Deacon remained silent for a moment as if in deep thought; then rising up suddenly said, *'If God be for me, who can be against me.* If Alexander Campbell is a man of God, an agent of the truth, and I have never yet ceased to believe that he is, I have no fears, and let me tell you this—you will hear something Wednesday night the like of which you have never heard before. You will hear a man who is not to be wheedled and brow-beaten by a few hot-headed alarmists, but who can stand before an Edinburgh audience with as little fear as Paul before Agrippa. You will not hear a silver-tongued orator, a dramatic actor, sniffing and weeping to play upon the cords of sympathy, but a second John Knox of whom it may be said, while he is yet living he does not fear the face of man.' Having said this brother Morton left me.

"Wednesday evening at seven o'clock found me in Waterloo Rooms. The vast auditorium was then filling, nearly an hour before the great American was to be heard. I succeeded in securing a good sitting for myself, in the right of the room, about forty feet from the platform. The audience now in their seats numbering upward of three thousand were quiet, little talking was done; all eyes were intent upon the rostrum, though the time for the appearance of the speaker was over half an hour ahead. The crowd kept pouring in— the room got hot and stifling, and the only sound was that of waving fans. Fifteen minutes more passed, and every seat in the whole hall was filled, but the crowd seeking entrance seemed increasing. All standing room was soon taken, and before the hour of eight arrived, every available space in the whole building into which a human being could crowd himself was packed. Interest became intense —but hardly a word was said. The rooms which now held between 6,000 and 7,000 people grew hotter and closer. The word is given that a woman has fainted in the rear, but we all hold our seats. Now some one on the left cries out 'Air! Let us have some ventilation.' This suggests a response from the far rear, where someone cries out, 'There is likely to be more ventilation than some of us care for before this meeting closes.' This was greeted by a hearty 'Hear! Hear!' from all quarters of the audience. It sounded good. It looked as if this audience had some Campbell men in it who were not afraid to show their colors, and who were informed of the trickery of his enemies. I was now almost a Campbell man myself—the only thing I feared from him was his religious teaching. At this moment the door at the rear of the rostrum slightly creaks on its hinges, and all is hushed —every eye is strained in that direction. But it closes, and we are left again in suspense."

"A Man who Stood Head and Shoulders Above All that were in the House."

It may now be interesting for us to recapitulate for a moment. Let us raise our heads, look about us, and see where we find ourselves. The Midland train had been rushing at a rapid rate through England, while my friend was rehearsing to me his interesting narrative. We had passed through many important manufacturing towns on our way. After leaving Bedford, but a few miles further on, stood the old hamlet of Olney some distance from the railroad. Here is where the poet Cowper lived in a family of very devout Methodists, and where he wrote his principal poetical works and religious hymns. It was here that he wrote "The Task" on the suggestion of a lady friend, that he should compose a poem about the sofa on which she was sitting. This was "the task" that she gave him. Here he also composed that popular ballad, "John Gilpin's Ride." But among religious people Cowper is known more as a psalmist. While yet a young man, he lost his mind, because of the great fright with which he anticipated the approach of an occasion on which he was to appear before court as a judicial reader. Upon the recovery of his reason, his temperament, which had before been skeptical and reckless, was changed—he was intensely religious, and as this was just the time of the great Methodist revival, he joined the Wesleyans and became the great poet of Methodism, as Milton had been of Puritanism. His hymns are nighty evangelical in spirit and eminently orthodox in tone, as the following well known verse will show:

> *There is a fountain filled with blood,*
> *Drawn from Immanuel's veins,*
> *And sinners plunged beneath that flood,*
> *Lose all their guilty stains.*

Such a mode of expression sounds rather vulgar to us now; its language is grossly material and even coarse, but it was such language as this that characterized the great Methodist revival, and was, to a great extent, the source of its power with the lower classes.

So profound had been my interest in my friend's narration, that in all the long distance from Bedford northward, I was hardly conscious of what we passed. With all the beautiful and varied scenery which the route ran through, —the rocky, rough and hilly land from Leeds northward—the antique looking stone houses, the beautiful stone fences built without mortar, and winding about the hills and mountain sides, the green and well-kept hedges, which took the place of the stone fences from Appleby on; with all this and much more, the route had not impressed me either one way or the other, and had not my return over the same road given me an opportunity to see what I had missed, I never would have known what that trip contains. Such was the interest of the story to which I was listening that I had seen and not seen like the village girl in *Enoch Arden,* "Who sets her pitcher underneath the spring, hears and not hears and lets it overflow."

At the point of the narrative where the last paper closed, we had just left Carlisle, on the borders, and were rushing on toward Edinburgh through the Scottish lowlands. Again we resume the story where we last left our friend:

"The vast multitude crowded in that largest auditorium in Edinburgh was getting restless and nervous—about seven thousand people, all drawn there by a lively interest, whether of curiosity or personal admiration, or desire for Christian enlightenment, were now awaiting the appearance of the famous American. At just 8 o'clock the door at the rear of the platform again opened, and Alexander Campbell, accompanied by a gentleman I did not know, advanced toward the audience. They seated themselves, and the gentleman who was with him, leaned over and whispered to Mr. Campbell. The latter, without taking his eyes off the audience, which he had been scanning with swift, flashing, eagle glances, nodded approval, and his companion arose and stood before the assembly to make the introductory speech. What he said I cannot remember—I doubt if anyone would have known five minutes afterwards, for all eyes and minds were chained upon the illustrious stranger, who, with an air of perfect ease, sat before us with one arm resting on the arm of his chair, and the coolness of his behavior betokening his full mastery of the situation. It was with no sign of timorousness that he took in his audience. That flowing gray hair solicited our reverence, that dignified bearing commanded our respect, those keen dark eyes shining from under an intellectual forehead and heavy eyebrows, filled us with a certain admiration and awe. This man would be no humble petitioner for our grace—he would not play upon our passions, nor stoop to the exercise of the orator's trick to gain our favor and sympathy. From the moment I set my eyes upon him, my previous impressions vanished—this was not the Alexander Campbell whom I had seen in fancy. A like change came over the minds of the audience. A murmur of surprise and admiration went through the whole house, when he sat down.

"A whisper behind me, which I overheard, will represent the first impression with which Alexander Campbell inspired that assembly. 'He is the Saul of this company,' spoke a voice just behind me as Mr. Campbell sat down and looked over the mass of humanity which lay before him. And this was the feeling of that night—here was a man who stood head and shoulders above all that were in the house.

"When the brief remarks of introduction were finished he arose and advanced to the front of the platform. He was rather tall, but firmly built. His complexion was ruddy and even youthful; but his hair was nearly white. His carriage was erect and imposing, but his pose was not that of an orator who has carefully studied pantomime and stands for effect. He seemed oblivious of his attitude; he had something to say, but no piece to act. My memory of his opening words is quite distinct.

"My Friends and Citizens of Edinburgh: It is with gratitude that I see so vast an audience in this room, and we shall hope, and surely our hopes will be fulfilled, that the motive which has brought you here is your desire to know the truth in whatever directions of it we may choose to follow. '

"These words were given in a full and rounded voice, and with a confidence and force which was calculated to quiet all opposition and question. Nevertheless, a great disturbance arose in the rear which had been previously arranged for by Campbell's enemies. It began with a simultaneous coughing and scraping of feet. The speaker's method of procedure during this annoyance was the best I have ever seen. He knew that the great majority of his auditors were curious to hear what he was going to say, and were anxious to catch every word. Instead then of stopping for the noise to subside, in which case a general hubbub would have been brought on, he continued in his cool, easy and interesting way of speaking, without raising his voice, or taking the least notice of the disturbance. In a few moments so annoyed were the remainder of the audience, who were hardly able to follow the speaker's thoughts in all the noise, that they soon hissed the roisterers into shame and silence. This was the great man's first victory—we were all now getting into sympathy with him. In the general quiet that followed the hissing, he caught his first chain of union that helped to bind him more to his audience; his face lit up with a renewed fire, and his expression took on a fuller vigor; he had been from the beginning master of the situation; he was now lord of all he surveyed. A gradually swelling volume of voice and thought began from this point. His well-rounded and finished periods rolled one upon another laden with thought, compact but clear, and logic, close and rigid. Not a sentence but the freshness of the thought, the force and aptness of the expression, the convincing logic that held it, surprised us. I have not a distinct recollection of what he said; not even of the line of argument which he pursued, but I see his form before me after the flight of nearly half a century as I saw it then, strong and commanding, quiet yet animated. I can hear again, as the rush of distant but mighty waters, the volume of that voice, bearing on its tide facts and arguments that seemed to place all things on which he touched beyond all peradventure. I can see once more that spell-bound multitude that sat for three hours under the matchless torrent of eloquence of the highest kind, inspired, as it was, by the occasion, the vast audience and the causes which had brought them there. One more attempt at a disturbance had been made early in the evening when Mr. Campbell was reading the letter he had written to the *Journal,* offering to debate with any man whom the Anti-Slavery Society might choose, on the subject of American slavery, even with the Rev. James Robertson himself, provided he was not the James Robertson who had been expelled from his church for violating the fifth commandment. At this point the cry of 'Libel!' was raised by some friends of Robertson, which suggested to him, no doubt, his subsequent course of action. But this cry Mr. Campbell treated in the same method he had used with the first disturbance, and it was soon quieted."

"A Sort of Confused Expression of Surprise"

The address of Alexander Campbell before an audience prejudiced greatly against him at the start, and composed of a people peculiarly difficult to work upon, was a feat of oratory such as has but one comparison in this century —that of Henry Ward Beecher in Liverpool. But there are points of difference between these two very similar facts in the history of oratory. Beecher's audience, in the first place, not so large, was not prejudiced against *him,* but his cause—of him as a man they knew little. The audience that met him was louder and more boisterous in its interruptions —it was of a coarser and more illiterate class of people, not so serious in its prejudices, nor so embarrassing in its opposition. There were many Americans who were with Beecher, and a large percentage of the assembly was in sympathy with him, and exerted its influence to quiet disorder, and render him encouraging applause. But none of these things were points in Campbell's favor. He had to face an enormous assemblage of intelligent people, wrought up to a high degree of righteous indignation and intense prejudice against him personally, they met him not with the tumult and uproar that confronted Beecher, but with that repellent expression of distrust and suspicion which is often more embarrassing and unnerving to a speaker than a riotous and noisy opposition.

But the calm dignity and repose with which he appeared before his audience, and the easy but respectful confidence which he manifested in himself, the supreme contempt with which he treated the interruptions that began with the opening of his speech, the entrancing power of his language, and the fascination and force of his delivery, made him master of his audience—they seemed to forget themselves and sat at his feet as learners.

Beecher is more human than Campbell—he was troubled by the hissing and mimicking that he received and sometimes even lost his temper, as where he said after a very exasperating season of hissing and uproar, "I think the bark of those men is worse than their bite. They don't mean any harm—they don't know any better." This was in harmony with Beecher's temperament, though not quite representative of his usual presence of mind, but nothing could have been less consonant with the tone and spirit of Campbell than to have shown such irritation. The Liverpool rabble received patronage for their coarse jests and sarcastic ridicule in the attention which the speaker paid to them, but there was no satisfaction to the interrupter of the Edinburgh orator; his carriage and demeanor, as well as the momentum of his thought and speech, and the positiveness of his personality made such frivolity and play very much out of tone. Beecher's speech, with all its interruptions, was an hour and a half long. Campbell spoke continuously for nearly three hours, and during that three hours a gradual but very complete change was produced in his listeners. They were not Goldsmith's "fools who came to scoff" and "remained to pray," but they were intelligent people who came as censors to listen to a criminal's attempt at self-justification, and then condemn him, but they remained as humble disciples, hanging upon the lips of one who had been to them the type of all that was unworthy. I refer to the great bulk of the audience, and neither to the friends, nor irreconcilable enemies of Campbell, who were there in large numbers, but composed only a small proportion of the whole assembly. Campbell was not greeted with applause once—it was a quiet affair. I resume my friend's narrative again as he describes the closing of the great meeting:

"At the close of the address, they seemed to remain for a moment in their seats, and turned with a sort of confused expression of surprise as they looked now for the first time in three hours into each other's faces—there had been a revulsion of feeling, and they seemed as if ashamed to talk with one another. Slowly and quietly they passed out. I looked over the mass of moving people, and there I saw my friend Robertson. He had received some very dispassionate, but rough handling by the speaker of the evening, whose power of administrating a dignified but smarting castigation I have seldom if ever seen equaled. There was a cloudy expression of evil in Robertson's countenance, mingled with the shrinking signs of humiliation and disappointment. He had been baffled. Alexander Campbell was now a hero, and he himself a villain in proportion. I could read his feelings well enough, and told Deacon Morton whom I saw smiling and exultant, as we were passing out of the door that the thing was not ended yet, if I rightly interpreted the handwriting on the wall, for Robertson's face did resemble a stone wall in its blank, cold determination. But we had no time nor opportunity for a conversation, for soon we were separated again by the jam. I went immediately to my lodgings in the city and retired."

Now while our friend Laird is enjoying his refreshing slumber after the great address which he has described, let us take a view of the religious situation in Scotland. Four years before this time the disruption of the National Kirk had taken place, and Thomas Chalmers, with 400 of the most pious and learned men of the old Kirk, went off and formed a communion of their own, since known as the Free Church of Scotland. This became at once a very powerful body, and has, since that day, contributed to Scotland a large part of the brains that gives her such a high status in the world of intellect. A wave of religious excitement had from 1840 and earlier passed over Scotland which did not spend its forces for several years. It affected all denominations. The following clipping from the *Glasgow Chronicle,* in 1839, gives us a representative picture of the revival mania in Scotland:

"It appears to have been understood among the revivalists that there was to be on Sunday, 'a great manifestation of the power of God,' at Kilsyth; and in consequence there were assembled in the village that day people from the farthest north to the English borders. Beds had been bespoken for weeks previous; but the accommodation was quite inadequate for the multitudes that poured in, and hundreds had to bivouac in the open air. Every kind of conveyance from Glasgow was taken up, and fares were inordinately raised. The creator number of clergymen present belonged to the Established church, but there were also Dissenters of different denominations—Baptists, Methodists, etc. The services began in the parish church at 10 o'clock in the morning, and in an open field soon after, where they were persevered in until 6 o'clock on Monday morning. They were resumed Monday at 10, and were continued through the whole day and ensuing night. A third time the vast congregation assembled yesterday afternoon, and we understand the proceedings were not yet at a close, and scenes of a most deplorable nature were exhibited. Nor was the language of the preachers calculated to calm the storm. One reverend gentleman told a portion of his audience that he 'saw the devil looking out of their eyes;' on which several women fell down insensible. On this, as on previous occasions, the chief actors in the scene were the clergy and the women. This revival mania (says a correspondent), has boarded our canal boats, and where formerly a blind old man might be found drawing a few pence from the compassion of the passengers, through the strains of his fiddle, we have now regular conventicles. Yesterday evening I came into Glasgow from Kirkintillock, in one of the canal boats, and was astonished to find a company of people engaged in religious exercises, with all the fervor peculiar to them. The service was led by a clergyman who gave out a Psalm which was sung by the followers (mostly women); he then prayed and preached in the revival strain. A number of the other passengers, conceiving that this mode of acting was quite improper in a promiscuous company confined together on board a small boat, exhibited symptoms of impatience, on which they were denounced as children of the devil and heirs of hell."

The religious fanaticism was a sort of epidemic that spread over the whole of the island. It was about this time—a few years later—that the outbreak of the "Canterbury Fanatics" took place. About the beginning of the year 1842, a stranger made his appearance at Canterbury, who attracted considerable notice by his handsome and commanding figure. He put forth pretensions to superior sanctity, and mysteriously intimated that he had a great work to do. The state of the public mind was such that devotees soon surrounded him, largely of the low and ignorant class, but also a few of wealth and respectable station. He passed himself off as Sir William Courtney, but his real name was John Thom. This man, though half-crazy himself, and a most transparent religious fraud, was able to put himself at the head of a multitude of followers, for he had persuaded them that he was the Messiah, and marching through the country in their lawless frenzy, they were repulsed only after much bloodshed and the death of the impostor himself. Nearly all human movements, though they be good on the whole, are likely to bear some of the evil fruits. These are some of the evil fruits of the great evangelical revival of the eighteenth century.

This general religious fanaticism gradually cooled down and was superseded by a deep and intelligent interest in religious matters such as was at the basis of the "Disruption" of 1843, and as gave a profound interest in the restoration of apostolic Christianity. Individuals here and there were breaking away from sectarian Christianity and seeking to realize the primitive model as developed in the New Testament; churches were heard from in different parts of the kingdom, which were already walking wholly in the light of the New Testament. Timothy Coop had trod the path of the Restoration alone, and had founded a congregation after the apostolic example before he had even heard of the Current Reformation. The movement of the Plymouth Brethren was a systematic attempt along the same line.

The picture of religious Britain for the closing decade of the first half of this century is one of exceeding interest for all these reasons.

"The Great Misfortune
of His Tour"

We have dwelt sufficiently upon the Edinburgh sensation of Alexander Campbell's Scottish tour—an incident of no little fame both here and in Scotland, even to this day. The religious principles of which he was the great exponent, and for the dissemination of which his British trip had been largely planned, had suffered greatly in the noise and excitement of this sensation—the public mind was too much engrossed by the personal troubles in which he was entrapped, for such a cool and deliberate consideration of his views as was calculated to make adherents to the system of truth which he advocated. The plans of his enemies had in a certain degree been successful. They had detracted popular attention from the principles to the man, from the work to the instrument of it, from the fountain to the channel, from the truth to the medium; and although Campbell was more than justified in the eyes of Scotland, so that even his enemies became his friends, the course which led to his arrest and from thence to his justification, though a course for which he was not in himself in the least at fault, was not propitious for the growth of his system of religious faith. Seasons of great personal, social and political agitation are most unfavorable to religious interest and activity. These personal troubles of Campbell were the principal cause of his failure to enlist the attention of the people to his Christian doctrines. But great social embarrassments and afflictions also unfitted the people of Britain for the hearing of religious truth in polemical discussions at this time. The Irish Famine was at its starving period. This great event held for the moment the profound attention of both islands. It was the theme of orators in the pulpit and on the platform, the subject of the press, and the great question of Parliament. Sir Charles Trevelyan in 1848 said in the *Edinburgh Review:* "The time has not yet arrived at which any man can with confidence say that he fully appreciates the nature and the bearings of that great event which will long be inseparably associated with the year just departed." "Ireland is in your hands," cried Daniel O'Connell, in February, 1847, the last time his voice was ever heard in Parliament, "if you do not save her, she must die." The queen in her message proroguing Parliament, in the summer of '47, said: "I join [with my people] in supplications to Almighty God that the dearth by which we have been afflicted, may by the divine blessing be converted into cheapness and plenty," At this time also Great Britain found herself in widespread financial distress. So complicated were her commercial relations that the abundant harvest which came in the autumn of '47 did not end her troubles. Chas. Knight in his history of England says that "in September and October there had been such a pressure upon the merchants and traders as had not been experienced since the great panic of 1825. Mercantile houses in London of the highest eminence suspended their payments. Corresponding disasters occurred at Manchester, Liverpool and Glasgow.... In October the alarm swelled into a general panic; the crash of eminent houses went on in London; in the country not only mercantile firms but banks were failing; the funds fell rapidly; exchequer bills were at a high rate of discount." As a result of these social and financial troubles, the political life of Great Britain ran high. The navigation laws were suspended in the spring of '47, the corn laws were repealed, and the protective duties abolished or reduced.

Such was the social, commercial and political state of Great Britain in the summer of '47. It was therefore an unfavorable season for religious reform. Yet, notwithstanding all this, very unusual and quite immediate fruits followed Campbell's preaching in Scotland. In this specific work, even cold and conservative Edinburgh was not behind the rest of Scotland. George Gilfillan in his *Scottish Covenant,* says that "Edinburgh, with all its intelligence is a cold, skeptical and heartless city. From the influence of Hume's atheism it has passed into the shadow of the modified materialism of Combe. Religion is indeed able to maintain its ground, but little more, and dwells too evidently in an enemy's country, sneered at by one species of philosophers and ostentatiously patronized by another, finding many partisans in all parts of the city, but not pervading it all like a transforming leaven." But in the face of all the obstacles that stood in the way, Alexander Campbell made a deep and lasting impression on the religious life of Edinburgh. There is there to this day a strong, influential, and intelligent body of Disciples, which we visited last summer, but which, if it had been of any other shade of faith, would, by all that has worked against it, have been long since in its grave. Campbell, with all the detractions and difficulties which he met in that city, left his followers (if we may so speak of them) greatly strengthened in intellectual and social influence, and stronger, I believe, than they are comparatively today. From Edinburgh he visited the other important cities in Scotland, filling his previously made appointments and complying with as many of the numerous calls which came to him, as his appointed time would permit. But in this we shall not follow him, as nothing eventful marked his journey till we find him in Glasgow, where the great misfortune of his tour, and, as we might say, of his life, befell him.

Apropos to the remarks I have made upon the religious condition of Britain in the last decade of the first half of the present century, I wish to quote from Dr. Robert Baird's *Religion in America,* a work of eight books, first published in Edinburgh in 1843, four years before Campbell visited that land. This work was immediately translated into French, German, Swedish and Dutch "and obtained a wide circulation on the continent as well as in the British Isles." Dr. Baird was an American writing for Europeans. The work was revised in 1855, and his statistics were brought up to that time. He ranks the "Disciples of Christ, or Reformers, as they call themselves, or Campbellite, as they are most commonly called by others," as one of the smallest Baptist denominations. "It is," says he, "with some hesitation that, by placing these in this connection, I rank them among the evangelical Christians. I do so because their creed, taken as it stands in written terms, is not heterodox. Not only do they not deny, but in words their creed affirms the doctrine of the Trinity, of salvation by the merits of Christ, and the necessity of the regenerating or sanctifying influences of the Holy Spirit. Yet, I understand that there is much about their preaching that seems to indicate that all that they consider necessary to salvation is little if anything more than a speculative, philosophical faith in connection with immersion as the only proper mode of baptism; so that there is little after all of that 'repentance toward God' and 'faith toward our Lord Jesus Christ,' which are the indispensable terms of the Gospel."

"And what does Dr. Campbell propose to do?" our author further enquires. He then answers his own query in the following quotation from Campbell himself. "Simply 'to ascertain from the Holy Scriptures, according to commonly-received and well-established rules of interpretation, the ideas attached to the leading terms and sentences found in the Holy Scriptures, and then use the words of the Holy Spirit in the apostolic acceptation of them!' But let us hear him further: 'By thus expressing the ideas communicated by the Holy Spirit in the terms and phrases learned by the Apostles, and by avoiding the artificial and technical language of scholastic theology, they propose to restore a pure speech to the household of faith.' And in this way they expect to put an end to all divisions and disputes and promote the sanctification of the faithful. And all this is proposed by those who reject all creeds for churches; excepting, indeed, that which consists in making the Bible speak theirs! However plausible it may be to talk in this way all church history has shown that there is no more certain way of introducing all manner of heresy than by dispensing with all written creeds and formularies of doctrine, and allowing all who profess to believe in the Bible, though attaching any meaning to it they please, to become members of the church. [Now here comes a prophecy]. For a while, possibly this scheme may seem to work well, but before half a century has passed, all manner of error will be found to have entered and nestled in the House of God." How well this prophecy has been verified those who have been eye-witnesses of the growth in faith and works of this religious community for the last half century (for it has been nearly a half century since these words were written) can testify. There is not today a more intelligently and rationally orthodox people in this country than the Disciples of Christ. The philosophy of Dr. Baird and that of Alexander Campbell have been weighed in the balance that Dr. Baird selected—a half century's experience—and the former has been found wanting. The principles of the great reformer have stood the test. If our fathers fifty years ago could have foreseen this, many thousands more would today have been walking with us. Then after speaking briefly upon the character of the faith "it is not difficult to see that churches may soon be gathered, in which there will be but little true religion."

"It is on this account," he continues, "that evangelical Christians in America, Baptists as well as Pedobaptists, have many fears about Dr. Campbell and his followers. It is believed, however, that as yet there are not a few sincerely pious people among his congregations, who have been led away by his plausible representations respecting the evil of creeds. Time can only show the issue."

"The Heresy Trial of Solomon Morton"

Having spoken thus at length on the religious spirit that prevailed at the time of Campbell's visit to Scotland, and the ideas concerning him and his work that had been previously published abroad, we shall resume the thread of our friend's narrative.

"After the Edinburgh meeting I was particularly interested in Mr. Campbell's movements. His victory over the Edinburgh audience was local, not general. It served rather to unite his enemies and intensify their bitterness for him. 'Campbellism,' which had before been but a harmless delusion became in the danger that now threatened Scotland's religious peace, a 'damnable heresy.' No man now defended Alexander Campbell, the arch-heretic from this on, with impunity. In my own congregation there had been many who held views similar to those preached by Campbell and who had even advocated them before his coming, but they were quiet now unless they dared to face the music. Among these daring ones was Solomon Morton. Heresy had been whispered against him before— now it was loud, since he was fearless in his defense of Campbell and his views. I tried as much as I thought prudent to shield my friend, but he had become so fully converted to the new ideas (or the old ones as he used to call them) that he could not refrain from openly expressing his confidence in them. This was going a little too far, and against my earnest action, he was brought to trial, charged with 'holding doctrines contrary to the teachings of the Holy Spirit and perilous to be held both for the soul's salvation and the safety of God's church.' I tried very hard to prevail upon Morton to retract, but he firmly held his ground. The day for trial came—it was held in the vestry of the church and many ecclesiastical dignitaries from abroad were there to witness the first trial for the Campbellistic heresy. It began at ten o'clock. After a prayer by a visiting preacher the proceedings of the day began. The presiding presbyter stated the purpose of the meeting, and the general charge, which we have mentioned, was read, and followed by a warm discussion on the part of his prosecutors. He was accused of sympathizing with slavery and man-stealing, of holding doctrines not in consonance with the Westminster Confession, of having discarded the Presbyterian name, and of many other things which made him unworthy of further Christian communion. Morton was then called out to answer these charges. He came forward, took out his Bible and opened it. Just then one of the prosecutors arose and reminded the chairman that a categorical answer should be required of the heretic on trial, he should respond 'yes' or 'no' to every separate accusation. The injustice of such a requirement was obvious, and, besides, it was contrary to the custom the Scottish Church had always observed. I immediately arose and objected to such a course of action as unworthy of the church and as likely to do us more harm in the eyes of our people than all the protection it could be in this case. I trusted we were not so fearful of Morton in his use of Scripture that we could not accord him such a hearing as heretics had always been afforded. At this, one of the prosecutors responded that permission should not be given anyone to desecrate the Word of God by using it in support of heretical notions. 'We are all convinced,' said he, 'of his heresy. I move that we proceed at once to a vote.' Deacon Morton then spoke: 'Brethren,' said he, 'is this a matter in which I am to have nothing to say? Am I to be condemned upon the testimony of others, who cannot, by the nature of things, possess quite as accurate knowledge of the state of my heart and mind as I possess myself? I have been charged with sympathizing with and believing in certain things. Full and unhindered testimony has been rendered in this matter by others. Is not my testimony on a subject concerning which I claim to be as well informed as they, worth something, and can they not accord me as much patience, *while I defend myself as* I have given them *while they were accusing me?* I ask, will you hear my testimony on this subject?' After some discussion, Morton was voted ten minutes in which to make his reply. 'The specific, written charge against me,' said he, 'is that I hold doctrines contrary to the teaching of the Holy Spirit. To this much I can give a categorical answer. I hold the words of the Holy Spirit in my hand. I deny that I cherish one doctrine contrary to the teaching of this book. Let my accusers specify one and I shall humbly retract it in your presence today. This answer covers the whole of the written charge, for if my doctrines are not contrary to the teachings of the Holy Spirit, they cannot be 'perilous to the soul's salvation' nor to the safety of God's church. I deny the charge until more definite accusations are made. Wherein do I offend the Holy Spirit? It has been said today that I sympathize with slavery. For this charge there is no foundation, and I hardly need take the trouble to deny it. It has been also said that I do not respect the Westminster confession. I frankly own that it exercises no power over my convictions. If it is the voice of the Holy Spirit, then have I offended against God, but if it is not the voice of Holy Spirit, why should you or I respect its *spiritual* dominion over us? I ask you, is it the voice of the Holy Spirit? If so, then, it have I offended. If not, then surely I have avoided that same offence in refusing to place it in the throne of the Holy Spirit, an offence which you commit, and not I. The only question, therefore, which determines whether heresy lies on your side or on mine, is whether the Westminster creed is the voice of the Holy Spirit.

"'I have also been charged with rejecting the Presbyterian name. Show me where such a rejection is contrary to the teachings of the Holy Spirit, and again I shall own my fault and abjure my heresy. Again the point upon which our respective orthodoxy is to be hung is whether the Presbyterian name has been applied to us by the Holy Spirit. If it has, then am I a heretic for rejecting it; if not, then you are the heretics for assuming it. '

There was no response to anything that Morton had said. He was called down by the chairman on the second, but his ten minutes had been sufficient. His prosecutors became more rabid in their remarks, but the more reasonable portion of the session considered him with some favor. The vote was taken and by a plurality of two votes against him he was pronounced a heretic. This trial did us more harm than anything else that had happened to us. It was universally condemned as an outrage and such a reaction followed that several of our best members went with Morton and joined the Disciples in Edinburgh. It was the first and last trial for heresy of Campbellism that was ever precipitated upon a Scottish Kirk-session to my knowledge."

Just as my friend Laird was concluding his account of the heresy trial of Solomon Morton, the Midland train which we had taken that morning from London, went thundering into the Edinburgh depot. He was met at the train by his family, and after introducing me to them, he urged me very earnestly to go with him to his home and accept his hospitality while in Edinburgh, hoping, as he said, that we might have an opportunity of further conversing on this theme, which was so interesting to him. But as my traveling plan did not favor my accepting his invitation, I begged to decline, and, hastily bidding each other good-bye, we were soon lost in the jam that gathered upon the platform. I watched him with a feeling of strange loneliness as his tall form and flowing hair vanished from my sight in the evening twilight. I had learned much from him; he had given my young hero-worshiping enthusiasm a wider field of action; he had given me a straightforward record, honest and simple, of some sad experiences in a great man's life; a kind old man he was and now I should see him no more. The narrative of John Laird is ended, but the saddest trial of our Reformer is yet to be told.

"I have Known and Heard Alexander Campbell"

It has been said by a certain writer that Campbell's "journey through Scotland was more like a triumphal march of a conquering hero than that of a preacher of the gospel." In this statement there is much truth; Aberdeen, Dundee, Montrose, Glasgow and all the great cities of Scotland which he visited, paid him such distinction as had been seldom showed to any American. But through his whole journey there was much unpleasantness; at every point he stopped, he found that the great red placards to which we have referred, had preceded him, forwarded from Edinburgh by Robertson and his colleagues.

After leaving John Laird at Edinburgh, my journey was chiefly among the Highlands, and I had little chance of seeing anyone who might draw out to its end the broken thread of his narrative. But in my diary I find the following memorandum:

"July 24. —Came from Oban last night on steamer 'Clansman,' had another interesting talk with a man about Campbell, landed at Greenock, proceeded to Glasgow."

July 23, we had left in the morning for a sail along the Ross of Mull to the ancient island of Iona or Icolmkill, and the not less interesting island of Staffa, returning to Oban in the evening. In this trip was a Glasgow shoe merchant, who was spending his summer in this popular resort. He was an old man of fine presence; he had the stature and manner of a Highlander. I enjoyed his intelligent conversation. On the following morning, when I boarded the "Clansman" for Greenock, this gentleman was on board. We immediately recognized each other and gradually fell into conversation. Our discourse turned on America and Americans, then upon religion in Scotland and America. I freely expressed my views as to the most feasible solution of denominational difficulties, and to my surprise he echoed my sentiments. Here is a man, thought I, who, like many others that are not informed of the movement toward Christian union, now in progress along this line, sees the ideal beauty of the scheme, and seizes the conception with enthusiasm. I thought it would be interesting to him to know that a definite movement had taken up this thought, and was bringing it out of the regions of abstract theory into the clear light of life and practice. I told him of the Disciples in America, and referred him to the work of Alexander Campbell, of whom, as I said, he might have heard. He heard me patiently through, and then with a smile, asked me if I had ever seen and known the great man whose name I had mentioned. My reply, that Campbell had died before my birth sufficiently answered his question.

"Then, possibly," said he, "I can tell you something about him. I have known and heard Alexander Campbell."

Once more I was a learner, and, begging him to relate his reminiscences of the great Reformer, which he began with interesting earnestness, I listened.

"The summer of 1847," he began, "is one I shall not soon forget. I had been a member of the Free church in Paisley—a young man just starting in business for myself. I was not particularly religious in nature. In fact, I was considerable of a skeptic. I was twenty-two years old that summer, and engaged to be married to a young lady of fine family, intelligence and beauty. Her name was Jeanette Craig. She was a member of the Congregational church, which was then one of the largest in the city. My skepticism, which I had not had the consideration to conceal from her, was, I knew, a cause of sorrow to her. Although she said little about it, she often handed me books and pamphlets to read, in the hope of staying the landslide of my faith. But none of these things had effect upon me. I was a great admirer of Robert Owen and his socialistic views as well as his infidelity, and one after another every dogma and article of faith as expressed in our standards vanished from my mind. I saw them go with sorrow and regret, but I could not help it; they were gone.

"Nothing had stood between Jeanette and me until the laxity of my religious views began to be whispered about, and Mr. Craig became alarmed at our intimacy, and, as I afterwards learned, told her she could never marry an infidel. For several months she had concealed the family opposition to my suit, all the time exerting her utmost endeavor to remove the cause of her parents' complaint. All her efforts in my behalf had failed. My love for her could not change my faith; her tears could not make real a truth which I believed did not exist, and I would not profess a faith to her which I did not possess, and I resolved to set myself about my own conversion, using every means in my power to honestly remove this ugly barrier.

"One morning," continued my informant, "as I was sitting behind the accountant's desk in the store, meditating thoughtfully upon the great problem of life, and the personal problem which was just then resting as a burden so heavily upon me, I received a package by express—it was a book. Business was dull, it being in the heat of the summer season, and I hailed with delight anything that seemed fitted to break the monotony of the dreary hours. I opened the package, and found the enclosed book to be the record of a debate between Robert Owen, my great hero, and a certain Alexander Campbell, of America. The book had been somewhat worn. Within the cover was a slip of paper, upon which were written these words, 'with a prayer for your conversion.' It was Jeanette's handwriting. I was sincere in desiring my own conversion, but I feared the issue of reading such a book. In Robert Owen I had the greatest confidence. Of Alexander Campbell I had never heard, with any certain knowledge. But I determined to give it a fair trial, though I had no hope of any change in my faith. Instead, I feared that this would complete its downfall. Jeanette had meant well by sending me this book, and for her sake I would do it justice. I commenced at the beginning; I read the whole account of the preparation for the debate. I read every word of Owen's introductory address. I liked it; I found myself back again, skeptic—in sympathy with infidelity, and almost anxious for the downfall of the great Christian superstition. But before I read through Mr. Campbell's masterly reply, my position was doubtful; I was not so sure that Owen could sustain his 'proposition.' The second address of Owen's was a slight disappointment; he had not been successful in answering his opponent's reasoning, and had for the most part avoided it. I became absorbed; the concision and force of the American's argument, the majestic flow of his incomparable style charmed me. His manliness and courage in attacking his opponent's reasoning, and his integrity in holding closely to the points in question as long as there seemed to be any hope in holding Owen to the same close work, called out my young admiration. The power of his logic was convincing. If I was any longer an infidel, it was not because I had not sufficient foundation upon which to build my faith. As for Robert Owen, he was a failure; his propositions proved nothing; he was not equal to the grounds he took; he stood as a dwarf in the palm of a giant's hand. Through chapter after chapter I read; the hour for luncheon came, but I read on; dinner hour came, and I was yet reading. I closed the book where Campbell, after having tried to maintain a close debate and hold Owen to the points in question, gives it up as a thing impossible, and lays out in an elaborate course of reasoning, the evidences of Christian fact— the basis for Christian faith.

"This day marked a *cross* in the history of my life. If I remained longer an unbeliever, I had nothing but myself to blame; I now had less as a skeptic to stand upon than as a Christian. I was happy; I felt like shouting for joy; the whole world looked bright; the gloomy clouds of unbelief had rolled away, and I saw clearly the full orb of the sun of righteousness. How reasonable Christianity was to me now! I did not need to read more. No barrier would now stand between Jeanette and myself; I could hardly wait. That same evening I went to see her and told her I was a Christian with faith as firm as her own—that she had wrought my conversion. The scene that followed I shall not need to describe. She called her parents, and before I left that night, the day was set."

"Alexander Campbell
had Done It!"

He continued:

"Imagine, if you please, my surprise when a few days after this I read a long account in the paper, of Alexander Campbell's visit to Scotland, and that he was on his way to Glasgow, and would, on the following Sunday, preach in the Baptist church in Paisley. I was elated beyond measure, and began at once to notify my friends, and tell them who Alexander Campbell was, but to my further surprise, I found that everyone knew all about it, and very few informed people were not familiar with the great man's name. My experience over forty years ago was what your own has been today.

"Every day's papers from this on contained accounts of Campbell—some favorable, some unfavorable, and some indifferent. Much of the week he lectured in Glasgow, and I went one night to hear him, but, getting there rather late, was not able to obtain entrance. Before Sunday came the people of Paisley were worked up to some degree of excitement concerning him, and his doctrines, his life and his Edinburgh troubles, but I remained his staunch companion through it all. Saturday night rolled around; crowds upon the streets were talking about the man who was to preach in the Baptist church on the following day. Someone stated that he was a slaveholder, but this was successfully contradicted. Another old Presbyterian deacon said that Campbell did not believe in the divinity of Christ and, he feared, would unsettle the faith of young people. Now was the time for me to speak *and I spoke.* One week ago I was skeptic; I was now a full believer; Alexander Campbell had done it!"

The next day was the Sunday toward which I had so hopefully looked. A bright and beautiful summer day it was—the air was cool and balmy. A half hour before the regular church service hour, Jeanette and I were on our way to the Baptist church. The vast house—for it was one of the largest church edifices in the place—was, even this early, nearly filled, and the crowd was pouring in. Everyone in Paisley seemed to be here whatever his church affiliations may have been. The pouring in continued—the ushers were compelled to pack the seats, and then a few minutes before the appointed time for the appearance of the speaker, chairs were brought in and lined the aisles. All eyes were on the pulpit—it was expected that the speaker would appear there. The fame that went with the name of Alexander Campbell, and the excitement in many places, that had accompanied this visit of his to Scotland, the prominence of the men who had felt it their duty to oppose him, and of those, also, who had espoused his cause as well as the reports and rumors which had flooded the land concerning his great power as a speaker, logician and theologian, had filled us with a sense of curiosity, which these few moments of waiting made quite impatient. Be not surprised, then, that a slight commotion and simultaneous turning of heads—even though grossly in violation of church etiquette—passed, like a wave, over the audience, when the whisper ran through the seats and galleries, 'There he comes!' I could not resist the impulse to turn my head slightly, and there I saw walking up the aisle three or four men.

"The first one was the regular pastor of the church, whom I knew. He was followed by a venerable looking man of commanding appearance, slightly above the medium stature, and firmly built. He carried a cane, but his motion betrayed not the least infirmity; it was vigorous and easy. He followed the minister up into the pulpit, and Was seated. I did not from the first take my eyes from him. There was a peculiar fascination in his face that I could hardly account for. He was not by the most common standard a handsome man, and yet there was an unusual strength and masculinity of outline in his features that was very striking. His nose was aquiline—the nose of one born to command; his mouth that of the orator and teacher—inclined to be large, flexible, and in easy control; it was not the set, firm and taciturn mouth of the man who says little, but means much, but it was the mouth of one born to instruct—of the philosopher who has an overflow of thought and the sufficient gift of speech to pour it out in livid and lucid streams. But his penetrating eye—how shall I describe it? It was not, to use ornithological comparisons, the dreamy, meditative eye of the owl as she slumbers on in her proverbial wisdom, but it was the sharp flashing eye of the eagle, as she views from her lofty aerie a wide expanse, taking it all in, in one quick grasp, and at the same time penetrates with the closest scrutiny into the most hidden coverts. So much for the face of the great man. After the opening services he arose and began his discourse. His text was I Corinthians 13:13: "Now abideth faith, hope, charity, these three; but the greatest of these is charity." He began by properly defining charity as love. The first division of his sermon was taken up in an elucidation of faith. Under his treatment of this theme I saw the subject grow up before my mind in a reasonableness and symmetry of form that made it a new thing; the entire audience sat entranced for the whole hour that was taken up in the discussion of this theme; the old mysticism enveloping faith, which had been thrust upon me by the irrationalism of the evangelical Christianity in which I had been reared, passed away—I saw the subject face to face; I was growing into the manhood of Christian grace and knowledge.

The second hour of his discourse was occupied in the treatment of the second Christian element, Hope, and nothing I had ever heard equaled the grandeur and sublimity of this theme under his master mind. Hope, alone, was now to me even greater than faith. He dwelt upon its beauty and its eternity—that even when all sorrow and affliction come upon us, the hope of God is our comfort. I remember I thought while he spoke, of that closing passage in the "Pleasures of Hope" by his own great kinsman, Thomas Campbell:

Eternal Hope! When yonder spheres sublime

Pealed their first notes to sound the march of time.
Thy joyous youth began; but not to fade
When all thy sister planets have decayed—
When wrapped in flames the realms of ether glow,
And heaven's last thunder shakes the world below,
Thou, undismayed, shalt o'er the ruins smile,
And light thy torch at nature's funeral pile.

Then followed the treatment of the third theme—Love, which even surpassed the others. It is very distinct now in my mind. Through the whole three hours of that long and remarkable discourse, not the least restlessness was visible in any part of the great audience even in that sultry day in summer. The time had passed away unnoticed. In the first part of the sermon he had leaned easily upon the pulpit, and through the whole discourse, he hardly made a gesture. He made a complete capture of the whole audience, and from that day Paisley was distinguished for the sympathy and support it showed him in his troubles."

"He has been Thrown into Prison in Glasgow"

"The Paisley sermon of Alexander Campbell completed my conversion. The debate with Owen had shown me the weakness of anti-Christian arguments—I was from that time on no longer a skeptic, but I was rather a negative Christian. This sermon was what I yet lacked—I went away from it in full Christian stature, a positive Christian I now was. From that day on Campbell was the theme of our conversation. Jeanette playfully called him 'our common father,' as he had also opened her mind to the light of Christian truth in a way she had never seen it before.

"What was our surprise and shock when the news flashed through the town of Paisley that he had been imprisoned in Bridewell! Various were the rumors that accompanied this intelligence. Some said he had violently attacked a venerable clergyman of Glasgow, and was arrested for slander. Others said he was in prison for assault and battery upon a reverend old Edinburgh divine named Roberts. Then the report was circulated that he was apprehended just when he was about to take boat for Ireland to flee the country, for some misdemeanor of his in Glasgow. As a result of all this gossip, many turned against him. I remember seeing a group of men standing on a street corner; among them was a man whom I recognized to have been a few days before one of Campbell's loud supporters— his name was Sandy MacLaren. He was talking with great earnestness.

'I had my suspicions of him from the beginning,' said Sandy, 'I was convinced in my own mind that he was a hard case and not to be trusted, but I said nothing. He has now turned out to be a fraud, just as I expected. I said to myself that God would bring him to justice, and this he has done. I now have the answer of a good conscience in the exercise of Christian forbearance, when if I had pleased to say

but a word, I might have opened the eyes of all Scotland to the wickedness of this man. But the like of him will always receive their just
deserts, and as for me I have played the Christian part, but I ask no
praise. God will remember us all according to both good and bad.'

"I could listen to this no longer. It gave me another set-back. If
such men as Sandy MacLaren were God's favorite children, I had no
desire for the paternity. I was a young Christian, and weaker than I
before would have admitted. The man who had dissolved my infidelity, and made me all the Christian that I was, had turned out a fraud,
and was lying now in a prison cell. If that man is a fraud, I thought,
it will not be difficult for me to believe that the Christ to whom he
leads me is also a fraud, and the religion he unrolled to me a vast
deception. In this state of mind I called at Deacon Craig's, and found
Jeanette sitting on a rustic bench under the shade of the garden tree.

'I have been reading,' said she, 'this great debate. If it were not
for what it has done for you, I think I should find it very tedious
reading. My! isn't our common father learned? and what big words
he uses! When I read his arguments, I forget all about the thoughts,
and am lost in the charming labyrinths of his language. He must be
very great! He certainly is no *common* father. But why do you look
so troubled? '

'You have not heard of the great calamity that has befallen Dr.
Campbell,' said I, 'he has been thrown into prison in Glasgow. '

'Alexander Campbell in prison! I don't believe it. It's a false report. What is he in prison for? '

'As nearly as I can learn from the papers, he has been arrested for
libel against Rev. James Robertson, president of the Scottish Anti-
Slavery Society. '

'Mr. Campbell,' said she, 'is not in prison for libel. There is persecution in this matter. I remember hearing my father and another
man talking about something like this a few days ago. Alexander

Campbell is innocent, and in a short time there will be a great reaction in his favor. Don't feel that you have been deceived. Christianity is true, and God yet reigns, and Alexander Campbell will be vindicated. '

"A few days after this I went to Glasgow, and visited the great reformer in his cold dungeon-like cell in Bridewell. I was presented by one of the deacons of the Baptist church in Paisley. The cell was crowded with visitors, many of them persons of distinction. The illustrious prisoner discoursed to them for hours upon all manner of themes pertaining to religious matters.

"His friends begged of him to accept bail, awaiting the decision of his case, but he resolutely refused. 'I would still be a prisoner,' said he, 'and I prefer to be a prisoner confined than a prisoner at large. I desire to see how these anti-slavery philanthropists, bearing upon their standard the watch-word of *liberty,* will treat a stranger wandering upon their shores. I threw myself upon the mercy of their president, whom I wronged, if I wronged any one. This man, thought I, will show me clemency, and even forgiveness, from the magnanimity of his profession. But his laconic word was: *Take him to jail;* and in jail I am. '''

It will be well for us here to recapitulate. We shall remember that when the challenge of debate on the slavery question passed between Robertson and Campbell, the latter agreed to it provided his opponent was not the Rev. James Robertson who had some years before been expelled from a church in Dundee, for disgracefully abusing his mother. There were several Rev. James Robertsons, and Campbell had reason to fear it was the same man. Upon this point Robertson based his case, and it was with great reluctance permitted to pass the lower magistrates. Therefore Campbell was arrested and imprisoned.

The Trial of James Robertson for False Imprisonment

Ere we return to the narrative of Donald MacBrayne, for such is the name of the man to whom we have lately been listening, a brief outline of the legal proceedings to which the arrest of Campbell led, might not be uninteresting. The arrest was an obvious abuse of the spirit of the law, which was designed only to prevent solvent debtors from fleeing the country—from "crossing over into Canada," in other words. But Campbell was arrested, thrown into prison, and had to wait the slow processes of the British courts. The facts upon which Robertson based his suit for libel, were obviously insufficient; any Scottish lawyer could see that no libel was contained in the words which Campbell used and no libel was intended, although if there is any time when one man would be justified in venting his wrath on another man, it was surely then. Everything that Robertson could say which was calumnious and mean, had been posted in nearly every city to which the reformer went. A libel suit of good dimensions could have been based upon these placards, with Campbell as the plaintiff, and Robertson on the defensive, but Alexander Campbell was not a man constructed on a small and mean pattern, and it is not likely that that libel ever entered his mind. But a serpent extracts venom where a bee might find honey, and the Rev. James Robertson saw libel in the gentlemanly but cutting letter to the *Edinburgh Journal.*

When the case came before Lord Murray, it was immediately dismissed by him—the facts were not equal to the complaint; but the reverend gentleman was not satisfied; he yet smarted under the castigation which he received from a man whom he saw growing in popularity and influence at every effort of his own against him. The case was appealed to the highest court of Scotland, the Court of Session, of which the great Lord Jeffrey, founder of the *Edinburgh Review,* was then judge. Here again we introduce our speaker:

"That the case was dismissed by Lord Murray as possessing not a sufficient cause for action was no surprise to any of us. Scottish jurists are justly famed for their integrity, and we were only impatient because every day made a change in the prisoner's health in the dark cell at Bridewell. A deep cold was taking possession of him, and the strain upon his mind and feelings was making its effects seen. He realized the whole horror of the incarceration, and with a Gethsemane sorrow, his prayer was, 'Lord if it be thy will, take this cup from me.' But with heroic courage he could also add, 'Not my will, but thine be done.' Day after day wore heavily upon him. When the news of Lord Murray's decision came to his cell, it was filled with visitors. The joy with which it was received, was unspeakable. Some even wept in their gladness. Campbell's face shone with new light, and his eyes regained their wonted life at the prospect of an immediate release. But this sunshine did not last long. In the evening of the same day, a certain Malcolm Sturme, a great friend of Campbell, came in. Malcolm was a man whose face was an open book. As soon as we saw him, we knew there was something wrong. 'Robertson has appealed to the Court of Session,' said he, 'another fortnight in this prison cell.' The indignation of those present began to vent itself in language expressive of actual feeling. But the prisoner was calm and self-possessed. Disappointment was plainly marked upon his face, but not a word did he utter which betrayed even the least resentment against his persecutor.

"Robertson's friends very positively disapproved of the appeal— in the first place, because they saw it was useless, and in the second, because the matter was taking too much the semblance of persecution, and the sympathy of the Scottish people was becoming aroused in Campbell's favor, but Robertson was not inclined to let go of the last hold he had and so the matter had to go through. I have heard it said that Lord Jeffrey, knowing that Campbell's imprisonment would come to a close at his decision, and knowing all the circumstances of the affair, having heard Campbell's Edinburgh address, accelerated the legal proceedings as much as possible, so as to reach the case appealed from the decision of Judge Murray. Hence Campbell's days in Bridewell prison were cut shorter than they otherwise would have been. Though Campbell came out of prison with the universal sympathy of Scotland, I have heard it said he was never the same man again. A heavy cold had settled upon him, and a fever was taking hold of his hitherto robust constitution. A man nearly sixty years old is too old a man for such treatment. He had come to his fatherland in the hopes of recruiting his strength, which the cares and activities of a busy career had somewhat shattered. A damp cell in Bridewell was no place for him. I almost weep when 1 think now of that old man, reviled but reviling not again, persecuted but speaking no evil of his enemy. He was not such a man as one would pity—he stood on a higher plane—but when I think it over now recalling his sufferings and forbearance, I feel that there is one thing that the world ought to start back and do over again. But he has been dead now for more than twenty-five years, and such reparation as was due him must be from the hand of Him who makes no mistakes."

The thousands who waited in Ireland to hear the great man who had first seen the light in their land, were to be disappointed. The appointments which had been made for him in all the leading cities in the north of Ireland, were destined never to be filled. That voice which had been listened to by many hundred thousands, was never more to be heard in the land which gave it its first utterance. Its great power was being forever undermined by the cold, damp walls of Bridewell prison. The tedious days wore away; the iron constitution which had withstood the storms of abuse, and calumny, and the arduous labors of a never-idle life, was now giving way. A few weeks more and the Rev. James Robertson would have been satisfied. But the decision of the Court of Sessions came in due season. The imprisonment of Alexander Campbell had been felt as the shame of Scotland, and widespread was the joy with which his liberation was hailed.

Here again we resume the thread of our friend's narrative:

"The audience which assembled in Glasgow to greet and hear Alexander Campbell after his release was one of the largest I have ever seen within the walls. The hall was packed to suffocation. For the first time in Scotland he faced an audience which was almost entirely in sympathy with him. The hectic flush of fever was upon his face. He arose to speak. Breathless was the stillness that awaited him. The erect form which had challenged the admiration of an unfriendly Edinburgh audience, was weakened; and the penetrating voice, to whose volume and charm the former victory had been partially due, would hardly do its bidding. All felt the difficulties under which he labored, and after a short effort he was again seated, and a doctor, a classmate of Campbell's in Glasgow University, was called to the platform. He immediately announced that the speaker was laboring under a high fever. The disappointed and sorrow-filled audience was dismissed. It was a silent dispersion. A few days later Alexander Campbell embarked from the land of his youth and education to return again no more. His sun had risen from behind British hills, but its last rays tinged an American horizon.

"The disgrace to Scotland was soon retrieved in the disgrace of the man who brought it upon her. The trial of James Robertson for false imprisonment resulted in his fleeing in shame from the land to avoid the satisfaction which the law would require of him, the very thing which he had made the ostensible cause of Campbell's arrest. He has never been heard of since and the weight of his own burdens fell upon the shoulders of his bondsmen. The fine which amounted to £2000 Mr. Campbell would not receive, but gave it to the Christian cause in the land of his persecution.

"Such is the conclusion of the whole matter. 'Justice and judgment are the habitation of his throne.' Though the great reformer lived nearly twenty years longer, it is said by those who knew him best that he never recovered from the sad experiences I have related."

While my friend was concluding his story, the "Clansman" was still plunging through the dark waters among the numerous islands of Western Scotland. The stars shone clear and bright. Unconsciously I had wrapped my ocean rug well about me. I looked at my watch; it was three hours past midnight, so interesting had been the history to which I had been listening. The air was damp and chilly. A faint silvery mist was beginning to besprinkle the Eastern sky when I went to seek a berth below.

My story is ended. The main facts, here touched upon, have long since passed into history. If these papers have served to add to the interest and better understanding of these facts, they have fulfilled the purpose of their writing.

ALEXANDER CAMPBELL AS A PREACHER

By Archibald McLean

Alexander Campbell as a Preacher

ALEXANDER CAMPBELL was a many-sided man. He was an author and editor. Sixty volumes have his name on their title pages. He founded a college and was its president for a quarter of a century. He taught regularly all those years. He was a defender of the faith as he held it. He had oral discussions lasting for days with John Baptist Purcell, a Roman Catholic bishop; with Robert Owen, of Lanark, the Secularist; and with several other of the strong men of their time. He had written discussions with skeptics, Jews, Unitarians, Universalists, Baptists and Pedo-baptists. These discussions covered nearly all questions relating to Christian doctrine and to church polity. Mr. Campbell was a man of affairs. He married and raised a family. He was the father of fourteen children. He managed a large business and made money. He served the state that adopted him. He was a member of the constitutional convention of Virginia. He sat in council with ex-President Madison, with Chief Justice Marshall, with Randolph of Roanoke, and with many other of the illustrious men of the old commonwealth. Mr. Campbell was a conversationalist worthy to rank with Luther and Johnson and Macaulay and Coleridge. He preached in most of the states of the Union, in Canada, and in Great Britain and Ireland. It is as a preacher that he is considered in this study.

Mr. Campbell was ordained January 1, 1812. It is safe to say that he was one of the best known and most effective preachers of his own or of any time. While he lived in Bethany, where his business was conducted and where the college he founded was located, he travelled much and preached everywhere. The announcement that he was to preach seldom failed to call together a throng too great for any building. When the weather permitted, he spoke in the open air to the thousands that assembled from near and from far. Much of his preaching was done on what was then the frontier. The Western country was sparsely settled. Religious privileges were not as abundant as they are now. The people were hungry for the bread of life. No man even in a metropolitan pulpit spoke to more intelligent or responsive audiences. Like most of the preachers in the wilderness, Mr. Campbell was an extemporaneous speaker. The pioneers liked men, as one of them said, "who could shoot without a rest."

Few Sermons Preserved

While making the most conscientious preparation for the pulpit, he wrote but little. Writing sermons was exceedingly irksome and distasteful to him. At that time newspapers were not as numerous and as enterprising as now; reporters were not as ubiquitous nor as accomplished. Because of these facts, few of Mr. Campbell's sermons have been published.

Only two or three have been preserved; and these are not verbatim reports. While he was in his prime it does not appear that it ever occurred to him or to his friends that those sermons upon which he bestowed so much thought, and into which he put so much of his life, and which he preached with so much power, should be taken down and printed for the information and edification of those who might wish to know more of his message and style and to think his thoughts over after him. It is nothing less than a calamity that those sermons which produced such profound and far-reaching results should have perished forever when their author died.

Mr. Campbell's sermons cannot be placed in evidence. The most that can be done is to gather up some of the recorded testimony of those who heard him. Fortunately, these are a great host. Some of the witnesses, whose words shall be cited, were eminent in their day and will be famous for all time. Some were his students in the college; they heard him often. There are no better judges of true preaching than a body of bright young men gathered from all parts of the world. When we are told of impressions that lasted for half a century and longer, we may be sure that the sermons were of exceptional excellence.

Impressions on His Hearers

Jeremiah Sullivan Black heard Mr. Campbell at different times through a series of years. Mr. Black was for a time Chief Justice of Pennsylvania.

Later he was the Attorney-General of the United States. He was one of the foremost lawyers and advocates of the nation. He heard Mr. Campbell first in his youth. Happening to be in Wellsburg when Mr. Campbell was to preach, he went to hear him. He took his stand upon the steps of the court-house. At the close of the sermon he found himself inside the railing and within a few feet of the speaker. He had been drawn insensibly and unknown to himself. He told Mr. Campbell how much he had been impressed with what he had heard. Not long after, Mr. Black made a journey from Somerset, Pa., to what is now Bethany, W. Va., to hear more and to make a confession of his faith in the Christ and to be baptized. Many years later, Judge Black said: "As a great preacher, he will be remembered with un-qualified admiration by all who had the good fortune to hear him in the prime of his life. The interest which he excited in a large con-gregation can hardly be explained. The first sentence of his dis-course 'drew audience still as death,' and every word was heard with rapt attention to the close. It did not appear to be eloquence; it was not the enticing words of man's wisdom; the arts of the orator seemed to be inconsistent, with the simplicity of his character. It was logic, explanation and argument so clear that everybody followed without an effort, and all felt that it was raising them to the level of a superior mind. Persuasion sat upon his lips. Prejudice melted away under the easy flow of his elocution. The clinching fact was always in its proper place, and the fine poetic illustration was ever at hand to shed its light over the theme. But all this does not account for the impressiveness of his speeches, and no analysis of them can give any idea of their power."

Ex-President Madison testified to the same effect. He said: "It was my pleasure to hear him very often as a preacher of the Gospel, and I regard him as the ablest and most original expounder of the Scriptures I have ever heard."

Robert Graham, sometime president of Kentucky University, and himself a most effective speaker, spoke thus of Mr. Campbell: "I can hardly express my admiration of him in every walk and employment of life. In the social circle he was by far the finest talker I ever heard; in the lecture-room, the most instructive; and in the pulpit I am sure he had few equals, and no superior, according to my standard. He charmed all alike, the old and the young, the educated and the uneducated. Indeed, no one could listen to him and not confess him to be one of the greatest men of his age. He had a style of his own, and always elicited the admiration of his hearers. He drew and held his audience till they seemed oblivious to the passage of time. I have heard him speak for over two hours at a time, and yet no one became weary." President Graham was educated at his feet. He heard "the old man eloquent" as a pupil, and later when his own judgment was more mature, and this is his testimony:

> *"Time but the impression deeper made,*
> *As streams their channels deeper wear."*

James S. Lamar, of Georgia, a prolific author and a gifted speaker, gives his estimate of Mr. Campbell as follows: "People would come from far and from near to hear him, some of them making a day's journey. Others would follow him from place to place, so as to hear him from day to day. The difficulty generally was to procure a house that could accommodate the crowds that flocked to hear him. The people admired him, loved him, hung enchained upon his lips, quoted him, trusted him, and spread his name and fame wide and far. But he was sui generis. He did not belong to that class that is commonly meant when we speak of popular preachers. He did not preach like them. He filled and moved in a sphere of his own. He seemed to have, and deeply to feel that he had, a special mission, an appointment from his Lord to do a peculiar and world-wide work. I believe that the divine Spirit so rested upon his soul that he lived and thought and preached under the sacred and solemn pressure of this conviction. If, therefore, he was popular, it was not because of the orator's art; not because he amused and pleased the fancy, or touched and stirred the shallow emotions, but because all that was holiest in men's hearts and aspirations, and most clear and un-clouded in their intellects, recognized the grandeur and divinity of the objects which he set before them; and they loved to move with his lofty spirit in the region where Christ was truly recognized as Lord indeed, and honored and trusted to His very last word and or-dinance as the true Messiah, the Son of the living God." This is the testimony of a man of taste and discrimination, of a man who heard Beecher and Spurgeon and the other popular preachers of their time. Mr. Lamar speaks of Mr. Campbell as a great man—God-appointed and God-inspired. He represents him as "a figure statuesque, colos-sal, mighty; a grand and masterful man; worthy of his sacred mis-sion, worthy of the great brotherhood whom he led into the light and liberty of the Gospel, and worthy of the large place which he will one day be given in the history of the Church."

Dr. Heman Humphrey, then president of Amherst College, heard Mr. Campbell twice. In his account of what he saw and heard, he said: "In listening to him you feel that you are in the presence of a great man. He speaks like a master of assemblies, one who has entire confidence in the mastery of his subject and his powers, and who expects to carry conviction to the minds of his hearers without any of the adventitious aids on which ordinary men find it necessary to rely. There were many fine and truly eloquent passages in the two discourses I heard, but they seemed to cost him no effort, and to betray no consciousness that they were fine." Referring to the second sermon, Dr. Humphrey said: "He dwelt chiefly on the two clauses of the text, 'Justified in the spirit, received up into glory,' and I cannot in justice refrain from acknowledging that I never remember to have listened to or to have read a more thrilling outburst of sacred eloquence than when he came to the scene of the coronation of Christ, and quoted the sublime passage from the twenty-fourth Psalm, beginning, 'Lift up your heads, O ye gates, and be ye lifted up, ye everlasting doors, that the King of glory may come in,' when he represented all the angels, principalities and powers of heaven as coming together to assist, as it were, in placing the crown upon the Redeemer's head."

Theodore S. Bell, then a young man and afterwards a distinguished physician in Louisville, heard Mr. Campbell preach a sermon based on the first chapter of the Epistle to the Hebrews. In that sermon the speaker dwelt on the divine glory of the Son of God, a theme upon which he was always surpassingly eloquent. Dr. Bell said: "I never had heard anything that approached the power of that discourse, nor have I ever heard it equaled since. Under the training of my mother, one of the most thorough scholars in the Bible that I ever knew, and of Dr. Fishback, although I then made no pretensions to Christianity, I was almost as familiar with the Bible as with the alphabet. But that speech on Hebrews lifted me into a world of thought of which I had previously known nothing. It has been forty-five years since I heard that pulpit discourse, but it is as vivid in my memory, I think, as it was when I first heard it." Wherever he spoke, he impressed people in the same way. One Baptist preacher said what many others felt: "I once thought I could preach, but since I have heard this man I do not seem, in my own estimation, to be larger than my little finger."

Campbell's Style

Mr. Campbell's style was his own. He did not aim to copy any of the famous orators of ancient or modern times.

One of the strong pioneer preachers of Kentucky told him that he was surprised to find in him an entire want of gesture and mannerism; that he talked as men commonly talk. Mr. Campbell told him that he had studied the arts of elocution, but had conscientiously refrained from making any use of them. "The apostles were sent out as witnesses to a certain great fact. Suppose that one of them should, in making his statement before the people, have plied his arms in gesticulation, stamped his foot in vehemence, and declared his testimony in the ears of the people in a loud, stentorian voice? But how weightily fell the words of those first preachers, when, with composure of manner, natural emphasis, and solemn deliberation, they spoke forth the words of truth and soberness." President Humphrey noted that there was nothing vociferous or impassioned in his manner. He said: "I think he is the most perfectly self-possessed, the most perfectly at ease in the pulpit, of any preacher I ever listened to, except, perhaps, the celebrated Dr. John Mason, of New York. No gentleman could be more free and unembarrassed in his own parlor."

Isaac Errett's Estimate

Isaac Errett, the founder and for many years the distinguished editor of the Christian Standard, spoke thus of Mr. Campbell:

> *"We have known him, in his prime, stand for two hours, leaning on a cane, and talk in true conversational style, with scarce a gesture in the entire discourse. But to a fine personal appearance and dignity of manner, he added a clearness of statement, a force of reasoning, a purity and sometimes a pomp of diction, a wealth of learning, a splendor of*

imagination, and an earnestness often rising into impassioned utterance, which clothed his pulpit efforts with a high degree of oratorical excellence."

There is a tradition in Bethany to the effect that, when the students went out to preach, they carried canes and leaned on them while speaking. In his later years Mr. Campbell wore a long patriarchal beard. The students encouraged their beards to grow long.

Style and Language

It was said of Mr. Campbell by a competent critic that his style was transparently clear—his argument perfectly understood and appreciated by all—and yet his language was largely Johnsonian.

"The Latin and Greek derivatives were so familiar to him and so wrought into the very fiber of his thought and mind, that, coming from him, they seemed not strange and foreign, but near and home-like. His hearers might not always have been able to define all the words he used, but they saw and felt what was wrapped up in them. Thus it was that learned and unlearned listened with rapture to his preaching, notwithstanding he was at no pains to accommodate his language to lower grades of intelligence. Not only did they hear with delight, but his thought was deeply imbedded in their minds, to be retained and treasured there, to be solemnly reconsidered and pondered, changing in many cases the very currents of life, and leading to a blessed and glorious destiny."

It was said of Chalmers that his delivery was the first and second and third excellence of his oratory. "On great occasions he was absolutely terrible. His heavy frame was convulsed; his face flushed and grew Pythic; the veins of his forehead and neck stood out like cordage; his voice creaked or reached to a shriek; foam flew from his mouth in flakes; he hung over his audience, menacing them with his fist, or he stood erect, maniacal and stamping." The effect was tremendous. Whitefield's preaching was as when the strong wind passed by and rent the mountains. Hume acknowledged that his eloquence surpassed everything he had ever seen or heard in any other preacher. He said that it was worth walking twenty miles to hear him. His elocution was perfect. "His face was a language, his intonations music, and his action passion." Garrick said Whitefield could make men weep or tremble by his varied utterances of the word "Mesopotamia." Whitefield had absolute control of the passions of immense audiences. "When he was in the pulpit every eye was fixed upon his expressive countenance; every ear was charmed with his melodious voice; all sorts of persons were captivated with the propriety and beauty of his address." Franklin was so delighted with him that he said he would rather hear him tell what was false than to hear anyone else tell what was true. Of Robert Hall it is stated that when he spoke, "breathless silence prevailed." As he grew more animated, five or six auditors would rise and lean forward over the front of the pews; a new sentiment or expression would cause others to rise, till long before the close it often happened that a considerable number were standing. The concluding appeals of his sermon on "Dead in Trespasses and Sins" were remarkably sublime and awful. Dr. Ryland hastened part way up the pulpit stairs, and while tears trickled down his venerable face, exclaimed with a vehemence which astonished both the preacher and the people, "Let all men who are alive in Jerusalem pray for the dead that they may live!" Duff left the pulpit as if he had been dragged through the Atlantic. His tall, ungainly form swayed to and fro, and his long right arm waved violently, and the left one hugged his coat against his breast, his voice raised to the tone of a Whitefield, and his face kindled like one under inspiration. He went home drenched with perspiration and wrung his clothes. Of John Knox it is affirmed that he seemed as if he would "ding the pulpit into blads and fly out of it." There was nothing in the least dramatic in Mr. Campbell's manner. He rarely made a gesture of any sort. There was no attitudinizing; no nervous flourishings; no pointing upward to the stars; no stretching forth of outspread arms as if to embrace mountains. He was seldom tender or pathetic. His style reminded some of the apostle as he reasoned with the people from the Scriptures, opening and alleging that the Jesus whom he preached was the Christ. It reminded others of the Master as He sat on the mountain or in the boat, and spoke as man never spake to those who sat around Him on the mountain or on the shore. When Mr. Campbell spoke, there was no gesticulation and no sign of perspiration and no beating of the pulpit. He did not alarm any by the way he pronounced certain words. His reliance for effects was upon the inherent power of the truth he was illustrating and enforcing, and upon the Spirit of God.

Beecher's Description of an Orator

It was said by Henry Ward Beecher that no one can describe to you the lightning flash of an excited eye, the thunder of a mighty voice, the manifold evidences of the surging feelings that roll out from an orator and submerge the hearers, as the waves roll in from the deep and cover the beach. Something of that kind was seen in Patrick Henry.

It is recorded that, attracted by some gesture, struck by some majestic attitude, fascinated by the spell of his eye, the charm of his emphasis and the varied and commanding expression of his countenance, juries lost sight of the law and the facts and their duty, and the judges bathed in tears perverted equity, and the people carried the orator in triumph on their shoulders. Mr. Campbell never sought to carry the minds of his auditors by stratagem or by assault. Nothing would have been gained by such a victory as Patrick Henry won over judge and jury. Mr. Campbell sought to inform and to persuade.

Effects of Preaching

Marvelous effects were produced by the preaching of Edwards and Wesley and Whitefield and Erskine and Christmas Evans and others, both in Great Britain and in America.

The effect of one of Jonathan Edwards' sermons was as if some supernatural apparition had frightened the people beyond control. They were convulsed in tears of agony and distress. Amid their tears and outcries the preacher paused, bidding them to be quiet that he might be heard. The reading of the text in another case caused the auditors to feel that they were slipping into the pit, and they seized the pews and pillars to save themselves. By all accounts, Edwards had some awful and electrical power. Speaking of the effects of the revival which grew out of his own ministry, he said that "nature often sank under the weight of divine discoveries, and the strength of the body was taken away." The person was deprived of all ability to walk or speak. Sometimes the hands were clenched and the flesh cold, but the senses remained. Animal nature was often in a great emotion and agitation, and the soul so overcome with admiration, with a sort of omnipotent joy, as to cause the person, unavoidably, to leap with all his might with joy and mighty exultation. Under the preaching of Wesley, some sank down, and there remained no strength in them: others exceedingly trembled and quaked. Some were torn with a sort of convulsive motion in every part of their bodies, and that so violently that often four or five persons could not hold them.

Physical Manifestations in Early Revivals

Hearers dropped on every side as if thunderstruck. Wesley speaks of one woman who was held in bed by two or three persons. "It was a terrible sight. Anguish, horror, and despair, above all description, appeared in her pale face. The thousand distortions of her whole body showed how the dogs of hell were gnawing at her heart." "Another tore up the ground with her hands, filling them with dust, and with the hard trodden grass, on which I saw her lie with her hands clenched as one dead." Another roared and screamed as in a more dreadful agony. Some continued lying on the ground for two or three hours, as if actually dead. Whitefield tells that on one occasion the whole church was drowned in tears; they wept and cried aloud as a mother weeps for her first-born. Another time the vast congregation was drenched in tears. When he preached to the colliers the tears made white gutters down their black cheeks. Copious weeping followed his ministry. Thus it is said that the people were so greatly afflicted that the room was filled with cries; and when they were dismissed they went home crying aloud through the streets to all parts of the town. Again he says, that shrieking, crying, weeping and wailing were to be heard on every corner; men's hearts failing them for fear, and many falling into the arms of their friends. Many were carried away when he spoke, as wounded soldiers are carried away from the field of battle. "The Word was sharper than a two-edged sword; and their bitter yellings and groans put me in mind of the wailings of the damned in hell."

In the great revival in Kentucky and Tennessee early in the last century, people fell like a log on the floor or on the earth or in the mud, and appeared as dead. They lay helpless and apparently lifeless for hours. In many instances the head would be jerked backward and forward, and from side to side, and so quickly that the features could not be distinguished. In this operation the head touched the ground behind and before. Saints and sinners were thus affected. Men cursed the jerks while they were thrown to the ground with violence. Some danced till nature was exhausted, and they fell prostrate to the floor. In addition to the jerks, there was the barking exercise, and the laughing exercise, and the singing exercise, and the running exercise and the falling exercise. It is stated that persons on the way to the meeting would bark like spaniels, and sometimes during the services they would start up suddenly with a fit of barking, rush out, roam around, and in a short time would come barking back. The preaching of Christmas Evans in Wales was characterized by the jumping exercise. To be sure, these were not the sole nor the main results of the preaching of these famous men. Souls were born into the kingdom of God, and saints were instructed and built up on their most holy faith.

Absence of Bodily Agitations When Campbell Preached

When Mr. Campbell preached, these bodily agitations were conspicuously absent. There were no swoonings or trances or roarings, no running against a wall, no beating themselves against the ground or tearing it up with their hands, no screamings or ravings or other evidence of mental derangement.

The effect was perhaps as great, but it was different. He talked to the assembled thousands as an advocate talks before the Supreme Court of the United States. There were no convulsions or contortions. But many of those that heard gave themselves then and there to the Lord. Others resolved to mend their ways and their doings. Others, still, went home to search the Scriptures to see whether the things they heard were true. The results of Mr. Campbell's preaching might be recorded in the language of the New Testament. "Many of those that heard, believed, and were baptized." Judge Riddle, speaking of his preaching and the effect of it, said there was no appeal to passion, no effort at pathos, no figures of rhetoric; but a warm, kindling, heated, glowing, manly argument, silencing the will, captivating the judgment, and satisfying the reason.

Ability to Interest

Robert Richardson, the biographer of Mr. Campbell, describing his power over audiences, says: "Nothing, indeed, was more striking than his singular ability to interest his hearers in the subject upon which he treated.

With this his own mind was occupied, and, being free from all thoughts of self, there was in his addresses an entire absence of egotism, and nothing in his delivery to divert the attention from the theme on which he discoursed. For the first few moments, indeed, the hearer might contemplate his commanding form, his perfect self-possession and quiet dignity of manner, or admire the clear and silvery tones of his voice, but these tones soon filled the mind with other thoughts. New revelations of truth, themes the most familiar invested with a strange importance, as unexpected yet obvious relations were developed in a few simple sentences; unthought-of combinations; unforeseen conclusions; a range of vision that seemed to embrace the universe and to glance at pleasure at all its varied departments—were as by some magic power presented to the hearer, and so as to wholly engross his perceptions and his understanding. While that voice was heard, nothing could dissolve the charm. Minutes became seconds, and hours were converted into minutes, so that the auditor became unconscious of the lapse of time, and his attention during the longest discourse was never weary. Without any gestures, either emphatic or descriptive, the speaker stood in the most natural and easy attitude, resting upon his innate powers of intellect and his complete mastery of the subject, impressing all with the sense of a superior presence and a mighty mind.

Voice and Emphasis

His enunciation was distinct, his diction chaste and simple, his sentences clear and forcible.

The intonations of his clear and ringing voice were admirably adapted to the sentiment, while by his strong and bold emphasis upon important words he imparted to what he said a peculiar force and authority. ... His power was thus derived, not from graceful action, gesture, nor from flowery language, nor elaborate or glowing description, nor merely from logical argumentation, but from his singular faculty of stating and connecting facts—of producing more novel and striking combinations of related truths, and of evolving the grand fundamental principles of things. Seizing upon these by an intuitive faculty of sagacity, he obtained at once the complete mastery of the subject, which he was enabled to disengage with the greatest ease from all its complications, as the experienced wood-man, skillfully placing his wedge in the heart of the timber, rives it through all its knots and windings, or as some Napoleon directs at various distant points large and isolated bodies of troops, whose destination cannot be determined by ordinary minds until the unexpected concentration of the whole upon a given point reveals the comprehensive genius of the warrior."

At Times Fervor and Power

While Mr. Campbell's style was conversational for the most part, there were times when he spoke with the utmost fervor.

Thus one of his pupils says that sometimes he was like a living fire or a sweeping tornado, forcing you to forget all idea of logical connection, and impressing upon you only the idea of power. At such times he spoke with a rapidity and fervor of utterance which literally defied phonography, and so enchained the mind and heart as to paralyze the hand that would otherwise have reported his every sentence. He convinced his auditors; he did more than that—he stirred them. On one occasion it is said, when he was addressing one of the most intelligent audiences that ever assembled in Kentucky, quite a number of highly gifted and educated men rose unconsciously to their feet and leaned forward towards the speaker, as if fearing to lose a single word that fell from his lips; and what made the case more remarkable was that many of them were public advocates of the views he was assailing, as being, in his judgment, contrary to the Word of God; yet such were the force, clearness and eloquence that he brought to his task, that even those who differed from him could not but pay this high tribute to his admirable powers of close thought, and of lofty and brilliant expression. W. K. Pendleton, his successor as president of the college, said: "His ideas flowed on a perpetual stream—majestic for its stately volume, and grand for the width and sweeping magnificence of its current. With a voice that thrilled with the magnetism of great thoughts, and a person imposing and majestic as his mind was vigorous and commanding, no one could hear and see him, and fail to discover that he was in the presence of one on whom nature had set the seal of transcendent greatness." While enriching his discourses from his vast stores of knowledge, and presenting them with great power, the impression of immense reserve of force was always left upon the hearers.

A Great Pulpit Orator

To some, Mr. Campbell did not appear to be a great pulpit orator. Whether he was or was not depends upon the meaning we give to oratory and eloquence.

Longinus said that an orator must have a vehement passion, a certain madness, a divine frenzy, breathing into his thoughts, and inspiring his speech. Aristotle gave it as his opinion that eloquence or oratory is the power of speaking on any subject that which is most persuasive. Whitefield had the "vehement passion." His sermons are commonplace. Apart from him they have little merit and little power. Those sermons that now seem so tame were, when delivered by him, like a volcanic eruption—like torrents of red-hot lava, that carried everything before them. When Chalmers rose to preach, the entire assembly set themselves for the treat that was coming. They were all eager and intent. Every breath was held, every cough suppressed, every fidgety movement settled. When the sermon closed and the great preacher said, "Let us pray," there was a hurried rush for the aisles and the doors. Those that came not to worship God, but to enjoy the fascination of human eloquence, did not care to remain for the benediction. When he was the lion of Glasgow, Chalmers felt that he made a mistake in going to that city, for he could hear of no good that was being done by him. He was as one that had a lovely voice and could play well on an instrument; the people heard his words, but they did not do them. The church that was so mightily stirred by the preaching of Edwards drove him out into the wilderness to preach and teach the Indians. Mr. Campbell attracted great audiences. He held them firmly in his grasp. He sent them away deeply impressed. This shows that oratory is no one stereotyped thing. If it be true, as Aristotle held, that persuasive speech is oratory, then Mr. Campbell was one of the greatest pulpit orators that ever lived. It was noted in his time that he spoke largely to men, to lawyers, physicians, teachers and editors.

Length of Sermons

At home Mr. Campbell spoke from an hour to an hour and a half. Abroad and on special occasions he spoke twice as long. He often spoke two or three times a day.

The length of his sermons was in harmony with the customs of the time, and barely met the expectations and wishes of the people. They were hungry and wanted a full meal. His biographer states that minutes became seconds and hours became minutes. The people were so entranced that they were unaware of the lapse of time. A noted Baptist minister said to a friend, at the close of one of Mr. Campbell's sermons, that it was a little hard to ride thirty miles to hear a man preach thirty minutes. His friend said: "It has been longer than that; look at your watch." On looking, he found that it had been two hours and a half. He said: "Two hours of my time are gone and I know not how, though wide-awake all the time." That was no uncommon experience. The people were so engrossed with the great theme under consideration that they forgot all else. His sermons were so clear in statement, cogent in argument, rich in diction, and forcible in illustration, as to hold his auditors in rapt attention to the end.

Textual Preaching

Mr. Campbell's style of sermonizing was as peculiar as his delivery. He did not believe much in what is known as textual preaching.

He said that half a century ago the greatest divine was the man that could bring the most doctrine and pronounce the most sermons from a clause of a verse. He told of a Scottish divine who preached a sermon to a company of beer drinkers from the word "Malt." The plan of the sermon was: First, explain the different figures of speech in the text; secondly, exhibit the fourfold effects of malt in this life; thirdly, declare its fourfold effects in the life to come; fourthly, deduce a few practical instructions and exhortations for the benefit of the hearers. In discussing the first head there were four topics suggested by the four letters—M, A, L, T. Thus, M suggested metaphorical; A, allegorical; L, literal, and T, theological. Under the second head there were four particulars setting forth the effects of malt in this life, and all suggested by the text, as follows: M, murder; A, adultery; L, lasciviousness; and T, treason. Under the third head showing the effects in the life to come were these, and all suggested by the same letters; M, misery; A, anguish; L, lamentation; and T, trouble. The fourth head yielded four exhortations and all based on the same text; M, my dear hearers; A, all of you; L, look diligently; T, to yourselves, to the text, and above all to abstain from the use of M-a-l-t liquors.

Another preached a sermon from the word "But." Naaman was a mighty man of valor, "but he was a leper." He spoke of the exceptions in human life. It was a trial sermon and very ingenious and eloquent. After it was over the officers of the church said to him, "Brother, you are a very interesting preacher, but you are not the man we are seeking." Another spoke from the text, "And." "Philip and Bartholomew." Yet another spoke from the exclamation, "Oh!" and said a number of pretty things about it. One spoke from the mutilated text, "There appeared a great wonder in heaven, a woman." Mr. Campbell could make nothing of such fantastic texts. He spoke on the great themes that run like rivers through all Scripture. His aim was to set forth what the Word of God taught, and not to prove that it is true, or that some notions held were true because they are supported by texts of Holy Writ. With him the Scriptures were authoritative and final. His purpose in all his preaching was to make known the mind of the Spirit. Our minister went to hear him to discover whether he was a Calvinist or Arminian.

Back to Christ

After hearing him, he was asked if he found where Mr. Campbell stood. He said, "No, I know nothing about him; but, be he devil, or be he saint, he has thrown more light on that Epistle and the whole Scriptures than I have heard in all the sermons I ever listened to before." He went back of Calvin and Arminius and Athanasius to the apostles and their Lord. He was a profound and life-long student of the Scriptures. His familiarity with the language of the Bible enabled him to employ its glorious expressions and beautiful similes with great effect. "It was from it, indeed, that his discourses derived their convincing truths, their inspiration and their grandeur. Bible themes, Bible thoughts, Bible terms, Bible facts, were his materials, and these he wrought up with consummate skill into intellectual and spiritual palaces of glorious beauty, in which every auditor desired to prolong his stay. For the embellishment of these he employed Scripture metaphors much more frequently than comparisons, but it was upon analogies that he seemed chiefly to rely for illustrations as well as for argument. These, constituting his chief imagery, were usually grand, far-reaching and wide-spreading. Scriptural facts, precepts and promises seemed to be connected with them as naturally as flowers and fruits with the trees of the orchard. Uniting with their means the present with the past, one dispensation or institution of religion with another, and earth with heaven, he enlarged every one's conceptions of the plans of the infinite Creator in the remedial system, and through his varied and striking associations of thought produced the most profound and indelible impressions."

A Message for His Generation

Mr. Campbell had a message for his generation. He was engaged in a movement that had for its object the union of the people of God upon the basis of the Holy Scriptures, to the end that the world may be evangelized.

He called no man master. He honored the long line of saints and confessors and reformers. He learned what he could from each of them. But he did not make himself a follower of any or call himself by the name of any. No one of these had been crucified for him, and he had not been baptized into the name of any one of them. He went back to Christ and to His inspired apostles, and set aside all human creeds and confessions and dogmas that claimed to be authoritative. His voice called the people back to Christ and to the teaching of the Scriptures as the all-sufficient and alone-sufficient rule of faith and practice. He felt that as long as Christians continued to rally around human standards there would be division and confusion and every evil work. He saw in Christ, and in Christ alone, the one true rally-ing-point for all believers. In his preaching he sought to exalt Christ: this was his sole and supreme aim. He held Him up as the only Sav-ior and rightful Lord of all men, and urged them to pay the most punctilious regard to all His precepts and ordinances.

Favorite Topics

Among his favorite themes were these: The coronation of Christ; the mystery of godliness; the glory and dignity of the Christ; the riches of the saints. On no other subject was he so eloquent and grand and enrapturing as on the glories, the majesty and superhuman dignity of Christ Jesus. The last sermon he ever preached was on the glory of the Redeemer and the completeness of His salvation. Christ was the core of all his preaching—His character, His offices, His perfection, His supremacy. The Messiah was his perpetual and his highest delight. To him Christ was all and in all. No other preacher ever held more firmly to the essential deity of our Lord. No one ever sought more consistently and continuously to set Him forth as the only hope of men and nations. To his thought Christ was the key of all human history. In his conversation this was the master topic. No matter where he began, he soon found himself talking about Christ and His salvation. As all roads led to Rome, so all subjects were connected in his thought with Christ. His conversation was relieved with bursts of eloquence which even his finest flights in the pulpit never surpassed. On his death-bed he asked of the friends that gathered about him: "What think ye of Christ? of His divine nature? of His glorious mission? of His kingly office, the sovereign Ruler of the heavens and the earth, the Fountain of universal being?" Shortly before his spirit left the scene of his toils and triumphs, someone remarked that the sun was rising. He answered: "But to you that believe on His name, the Son of Righteousness shall arise with healing on His wings." He felt what Tennyson expressed:

"Our little systems have their day,

They have their day and cease to be;

They are but broken lights of Thee,

And Thou, O Lord, art more than they."

Sermon on the Law

In his youth he preached a sermon in which he contrasted the Gospel with the law of Moses.

His text was: "What the law could not do in that it was weak through the flesh, God, sending His own Son in the likeness of sinful flesh and as an offering for sin, condemned sin in the flesh." The sermon was preached in the open air, to an immense concourse of people. Mr. Campbell stood upon a rock while he spoke. His plan was as follows: 1. Ascertain what ideas we are to attach to the law in this and similar portions of the sacred Scriptures. 2. Point out those things which the law could not accomplish. 3. Show the reason why the law could not accomplish these objects. 4. Illustrate how God has remedied these relative defects of the law. 5. Deduce such conclusions from these premises as must obviously and necessarily present themselves to an unbiased mind. He undertook to show that Christ is superior to Moses, and the Gospel to the law. He combated the idea, then so common, that in every conversion there must first of all be a work of the law. The sinner must hear the thunders of Sinai before he was in a condition to hear the pardoning voice of the Son of God. Mr. Campbell held that the Law of Moses was provisional and local. It was for one people and for one age. It had no glory because of the more excellent glory of the Christian system. He never denied or doubted the value or the permanency of the ethical element in the Law of Moses. That element was taken up and incorporated in the Christian system. But, as a system, it waxed old and long since passed away. The shadow gave place to the substance, the type to the antitype. Mr. Campbell was careful to distinguish the different dispensations. He spoke of the patriarchal as starlight; of the Jewish dispensation as moonlight; of the mission of John the Baptist as twilight; of the Christian dispensation, beginning with the reign of Christ and the descent of the Holy Spirit, as the sunlight of the world. The patriarchs had the bud; the Jews had the blossom; we have the mature fruit of divine grace. This sermon was thoroughly evangelical. But because of it, Mr. Campbell was tried for heresy.

Tried for Heresy

Some narrow men sought to drive him out of their communion. In the trial he proved too much for his opponents. They continued to persecute him for years. Thirty years after this sermon was delivered it was published. Mr. Campbell said that so great had been the change of public sentiment in that time, that no association would take exception to its doctrine. No man could be further from being an antinomian.

Teaching Summarized

Isaac Errett summarized Mr. Campbell's teaching as follows: "Christ, the only Master; involving a rejection of all human names and leaderships in religion. The Bible, the only authoritative Book; necessitating a denial of the authority of all human creeds.

The Church of Christ, as founded by Him, and built by the apostles for a habitation of God through the Spirit, the only institution for spiritual ends; logically leading to the repudiation of all sect religions as unscriptural and dishonoring to the Head of the Church. Faith in Jesus, as the Christ, the Son of God, and repentance towards God, the only pre-requisites to baptism and consequent church-membership; thus dismissing all doctrinal speculation and all theological dogmata, whether true or false, as unworthy to be urged as tests of fitness for membership in the Church of Christ. Obedience to the divine commandments, and not correctness of opinion, the test of Christian standing. The Gospel the essential channel of spiritual influence in conversion; thus ignoring all reliance on abstract and immediate influence of the Holy Spirit, and calling the attention of the inquirers away from dreams, visions and impressions, which are so liable to deceive, to the living and powerful truths of the Gospel, which are reliable, immutable and eternal. The truth of the Gospel, to enlighten; the love of God in the Gospel, to persuade; the ordinances of the Gospel, as tests of submission to the divine will; the promises of the Gospel, as the evidences of pardon and acceptance; and the Holy Spirit, in and through all these, accomplishing His work of enlightening, convincing of sin, guiding the penitent soul to pardon, and bearing witness to the obedient believer of His adoption into the family of God." Mr. Campbell's theology was preeminently Biblical and Christological and Christocentric.

A Great and Good Man

Phillips Brooks defined preaching as truth through personality. Emerson has the same thought. He maintained that there is no eloquence without a man behind it.

Mr. Campbell's preaching would never have had the influence it had unless he had been a great and good man. Moses E. Lard, one of his scholars and himself one of the most effective preachers in America, said that nature had been lavish to Mr. Campbell. "Physically, not one man in a thousand was so well endowed. Nature was in a fertile mood when she molded his large and sinewy body. Material was abundant and bestowed with no grudging hand. There was not a pound of flesh too much, nor a pound too little. As to resources of the mind, no word but opulent will describe him. Here he was preeminently great, in the true sense of the word. His head was faultless, the finest I ever saw." Mr. Lard placed him among the very first of the very greatest of the sons of men. Mr. Campbell's father was a profound classical scholar and a born teacher. He took as much pains with his son as James Mill did with his son, John Stuart Mill.

Education and Study

Mr. Campbell took a course in Glasgow University. He developed and disciplined his mind by diligent study. For many years he spent sixteen hours a day in his library. In this case, reading made a full man. In his discussion on infidelity his opponent came to the end of his resources long before the time came for closing. Mr. Campbell went on and spoke for twelve hours on the Christian religion. This is one of the most remarkable addresses ever delivered.

Perhaps no man ever knew Mr. Campbell that denied his greatness. It was said of Burke that no one could stand with him under a bridge in a shower without discovering that he was no ordinary man. As Mr. Campbell walked the streets of London, a man who did not know him said: "There goes a man with enough brains to govern

Europe." In his presence other men were silent, and left him to do all the talking. They instinctively paid homage to the power of his intellect. College men are quick to see and recognize a great man. They spoke of his majestic and commanding presence. After fifty years they still feel concerning him as they did while under the spell of his genius.

Character

No one ever called his character in question. His critics assailed his views; no man ever had enemies more in number or more venomous.

He was accused of all kinds of heresies. He was charged with holding views that were mutually exclusive. His reputation was without spot. His bitterest enemies failed to find a flaw in his character for truth, integrity and goodness. His life was above suspicion and above reproach in that fierce light that beats upon a leader of men and blackens every blot. No father could wish for an only son a career more splendid or more stainless. To those that knew him well he was most cheerful, gentle, genial, just and devout; and as dearly loved for his goodness as he was venerated for his greatness. Mr. Campbell lived in constant and conscious fellowship with God and with Jesus Christ.

Religious Life

Like Enoch and Noah, he walked with God. He was filled with the Spirit. He prayed with his family and with his domestics. He was never too busy or too weary for family worship. This was a cardinal feature of his household economy. He had little confidence in a piety that was not nourished and instructed by the daily study of the word of God and a perpetual habit of prayer. Thus sustained by divine assistance, he labored for fifty-four years with an energy and a fidelity never surpassed.

Concluding Testimonies

This study may fitly conclude with the testimonies of four men of renown. Judge Black said of him: "The life of a Christian man worthy of his vocation is a battle at best.

He of whom I speak contended valiantly for the faith once delivered to the saints, not only against natural allies of Satan, but against errors which appeared to be consecrated by the approbation of good men; creeds imbedded in prejudice; falsehood guarded by interest which the slightest disturbance infuriated. It was a war against principalities and powers and spiritual wickedness in high places. The little band of disciples that gathered around him at first, and the world in derision called by his name, were as literally the 'sect' everywhere spoken against as their predecessors in primitive times. To effect a great reformation under such circumstances; to convince large numbers against their will; to organize the believers into a compact and powerful body; to conquer the respect of the world—these are proofs of intellectuality and moral force with which only a few of the children of men have been gifted. To these qualities were added an unfailing courage, a fortitude that nothing could shake, a chivalrous sense of justice to his opponents and affection for his friends, second only to his love for the cause to which he devoted his life. What higher claims can any man set up to the character of a hero?"

George D. Prentice, the brilliant editor of the Louisville Journal, after hearing Mr. Campbell, wrote in his paper as follows:

> *"Alexander Campbell is unquestionably one of the most extraordinary men of our time. Putting wholly out of view his tenets, with which of course we have nothing to do, he claims, by virtue of his intrinsic qualities, as manifested in his achievements, a place among the foremost spirits of our age. His energy, self-reliance and self-fidelity, if we may use*

the expression, are of the stamp that belongs only to the world's first leaders in thought and action. His personal excellence is certainly without a stain or shadow. His intellect, it is scarcely too much to say, is among the clearest, richest, profoundest ever vouchsafed to man. Indeed, it seems to us that in the faculty of abstract thinking—in, so to say, the sphere of pure thought—he has few, if any, living rivals. Every cultured person of the slightest metaphysical turn who has heard Alexander Campbell in the pulpit or in the social circle, must have been especially impressed by the wonderful facility with which his faculties move in the highest planes of thought. Ultimate facts stand forth as boldly in his consciousness as sensations do in that of most other men. He grasps and handles the highest, subtlest, most comprehensive principles as if they were the liveliest impressions of the senses. No poet's soul is more crowded with imagery than his is with the ripest forms of thought. Surely the life of a man thus excellent and gifted, is a part of the common treasure of society. In his essential character he belongs to no sect or party, but to the world."

Bishop Hurst says that few men have impressed themselves more profoundly on the religious life of their age than Alexander Campbell. "His personality was of the most vigorous type, and for over a generation his name was a tower of strength over the whole United States. He was a man of purest character and the highest consecration. He leavened the whole country with his views. Few men have exerted a wider influence."

Referring to Mr. Campbell, General Robert E. Lee quoted the words of Dr. Symonds spoken about Milton:

"He was a man in whom were illustriously combined all the qualities that could adorn or elevate the nature to which he belonged; knowledge the most various and extended, virtue

that never loitered in her career nor deviated from her course. A man who, if he had been delegated as a representative of his species to one of the many superior worlds, would have suggested a grand idea of the human race." The New York Independent has said that there is not a religious body in Christendom that, whether it will confess it or not, has not been profoundly affected by his life and work. His influence and fame since his death have increased rather than diminished. It is believed by many that they will continue to increase till that for which he contended so long and so earnestly and so ably will be realized, and there will be one flock as there is one Shepherd. Coming generations will rank him among the greatest of the many God-given men that have blessed our earth.

DELUSIONS:

AN ANALYSIS OF THE BOOK OF MORMON

With an Examination of its Internal and External Evidences, and a Refutation of its Pretenses to Divine Authority

By Alexander Campbell

Prefatory Remarks

By Joshua V. Himes

It is well known to some of our fellow-citizens, that two preachers of the Mormonites, a fanatical sect, which originated a few years since in the western part of New York, have recently come to this city to propagate their strange and marvelous doctrines.

I have had several interviews with these men, and have examined their book, called the 'Book of Mormon', have endeavored to acquaint myself with the details of their history and principles, have put the result of my inquiries in writing, and am satisfied of the delusion and absurdity of their system, and of its evil tendency.

After this investigation, I felt a desire to have the system exposed, immediately in public print. But upon consulting with some judicious friends upon the subject, it was thought best not to take public notice of it at that time, as the system was so unreasonable and ridiculous, that no person of good common sense would believe it. But having witnessed the progress of the delusion among some of our respectable citizens, some of whom were considered worthy members of the religious societies to which they belonged, I have felt it my indispensable duty, to use my exertion against its spreading and contaminating influence.

However strange to relate, about fifteen persons, in this city have been led away by these false doctrines, have been baptized and joined the Mormon church. And some of these persons have set out for the promised land, the place of refuge for the house of Israel, and for all the Gentile world, who will take warning and flee thither for safety.[2] Two individuals who have gone, are defenseless females. They had acquired by their hard industry $2300, one of them having $800, the other $1500, which they have given up to go into the general stock. One of these females was in a consumption, and her friends thought she would not live to reach her destined place. Her afflicted sister told me, that if she had been buried here, before she had been led away by these errors, and had left satisfactory evidence that she was prepared to die, her grief would have been far less than it is now. The remaining persons who were baptized and joined the church, and contemplate going to the west, possess between $3000 and $4000, which they also are going to put with the general fund, and which they can never draw out again, should they get sick of Mormonism and wish to return home to their friends.

Thus are our friends swindled out of their property and drawn from their comfortable homes, to endure the perils of a journey about two thousand miles, by these ignorant fanatics; and when arrived at their earthly paradise, to become the miserable dupes of these temporal and spiritual lords.

In view of these evils, and after waiting impatiently for some time, hoping that some person better qualified than myself to do justice to the subject, would undertake it; but not hearing of any, I had concluded to publish the result of my inquiries of these men, with some strictures upon their book. But at this time I was informed by a friend, that a faithful review of the book had been published by one of the most able writers in our country. I immediately sent 600 miles for the review, and have received and perused it. In my apprehension it is the best thing that can be written upon the subject, and

---

[2] This place is situated in Jackson County, Missouri, ten miles from the town of Independence.

will be of inestimable use in preventing and rescuing many from the evils of Mormonism.

This review of Mr. Campbell came out first in the 'Millennial Harbinger', a monthly periodical published by him in Bethany, Virginia, under date of February 7th, 1831. This work is but little known to that class of persons whom I design to benefit. My object, therefore, in publishing it in a pamphlet by itself, is to circulate it among the people of New England[3] that they may receive the same benefit that the people of the south and west have, where the above periodical is extensively circulated. And I doubt not that its gifted author would not only be willing, but much gratified, in having it thus republished and circulated.

And with sympathetic feelings for those friends who have been grieved and afflicted in consequence of the delusion, and to prevent others from similar trials in future, by having their friends torn from their embraces, and swindled out of their property, and if possible, to prevent others from becoming the miserable subjects and dupes of these singular fanatics, I have determined to republish this review of Mr. Campbell, with these prefatory remarks; and would recommend the review to the perusal of my fellow citizens, and an enlightened public.

JOSHUA V. HIMES.
Boston, Aug. 14, 1832.

---

[3] These preachers intend visiting the cities and principal towns in New England.

Delusions

EVERY age of the world has produced imposters and delusions. Jannes and Jambres withstood Moses, and were followed by Pharaoh, his court, and clergy. They for some time supported their pretensions, much to the annoyance of the cause of the Israelites and their leader Moses.

To say nothing of the false prophets of the Jewish age, the diviners, soothsayers, magicians, and all the ministry of idols among the Gentiles, by which the nations were so often deceived, the imposters which have appeared since the Christian era would fill volumes of the most lamentable details ever read. The false Messiahs which have afflicted the Jews since the rejection of Jesus of Nazareth, have more than verified all the predictions of the Faithful and True Witness. No less than TWENTY-FOUR distinguished false Messiahs have disturbed the Jews. Many were deceived, and myriads lost their lives through their impostures. Some peculiar epochs were distinguished for the number and impudence of these impostors. If the people had fixed upon any year as likely to terminate their dispersions, and as the period of their return, that year rarely failed to produce a Messiah. Hence in the twelfth century no less than TEN false Messiahs appeared.

The year 1666, was a year of great expectation, and gave birth to one of the most remarkable of the false Christs. 'Great multitudes marched from unknown parts, to the remote deserts of Arabia, and they were supposed to be the ten tribes of Israel, who had been dispersed for many ages. It was said that a ship was arrived in the north part of Scotland, with sails and cordage of silk, that the mariners spoke nothing but Hebrew, and on the sails was this motto; 'The Twelve Tribes of Israel.' Then it was said that Sabati Levi appeared at Smyrna and professed to be the Messiah. The Jews gave up their business and attended to him. He obtained one Nathan in Jerusalem to pass for his Elias, or forerunner. Nathan prophesied for him, and the Jews became very penitent, and reformed under the expectation that the Messiah would appear in two years. 'Some fasted so long that they died—some endured melted wax to be dropped on their flesh—some rolled in snow—many whipped themselves. Superfluities in dress and household were dispensed with; property was sold to large amounts, and immense contributions were made to the poor. Though he met with much opposition, his followers increased, and began in large numbers to prophesy and fall into ecstasies. Four hundred men and women prophesied of his growing kingdom, and young infants who could hardly speak, would plainly pronounce, "SABATI, MESSIAH, and Son of God." The people were for a time possessed, and voices were heard from their bowels. Some fell into trances, foamed at the mouth, recounted their future prosperity, their visions of the Lion of Judah, the triumphs of SABATI.'

'When he was brought before the magistrates, some affirmed they saw a pillar of fire between him and the Cadi or Magistrates, and others actually swore that they saw it. This the credible Jews believed; those who would not believe in him, were shunned as excommunicated persons, and all intercourse with them was prohibited. 'The Grand Seignior, determined to try his faith by stripping him naked and setting him a mark for his archers; but rather than subject himself to this test, he turned Muslim, to the great confusion of the Jews.' We have been thus particular in giving a view, of the incidents of the life of this impostor, as a specimen of the others; and because of some remarkable analogies between him and the present New York imposter.

Numerous have been the imposters among Christians since the great apostasy began; especially since, and at the time of the Reformation. Munzer, Stubner and Stork, where conspicuous in the beginning of the 16th century.' These men taught that among Christians, who had the precepts of the Gospel to guide them, and the spirit of God to direct them, the office of magistracy was not only unnecessary, but an unlawful encroachment on their spiritual liberty; that the distinctions occasioned by birth, rank, or wealth, should be abolished; that all Christians should put their possessions into one common stock, and live together in that state of equality, which becomes members of the same family, and that polygamy was not incompatible with either the Old or New Testament.

They related many visions and revelations which they had from above, but failing to propagate their views by these means, they attempted to propagate them by arms. Many Catholics joined them, and in the various insurrections which they effected, 100,000 souls are said to have been sacrificed.'

Since the Millennium and the evils of sectarianism have been the subjects of much speaking and writing, impostures have been numerous. In the memory of the present generation, many delusions have been propagated and received. The shakers, a sect instituted by Anna Lesse, in 1774, have not yet quite dwindled away. This elect Lady, as they style her, was the head of this party, and gave them a new bible. 'They assert that she spoke seventy-two languages, and conversed with the dead. Through her all blessings flow to her followers—she appointed the sacred dance and the fantastic song, and consecrated shivering, swooning and falling down, acts of acceptable devotion. They are for a common stock, and rank marriage among the works of the flesh,—they are plain in their apparel, and assume the aspect of the friars and nuns of Catholic superstition.'

The Barkers, Jumpers, and Mutterers of the present age, need not be mentioned here. Nor need we detail the history of Miss Campbell, who in Good Old Scotland a year or two since came back from the dead and had the gift of tongues, who was believed in by several ministers of the Scotch Church. But we shall proceed to notice the most recent and the most impudent delusion which has appeared in our time. The people that have received this imposture are called,

THE MORMONITES. I have just examined their bible, and will first notice its contents. It is called the 'Book of Mormon', an account written by the hand of Mormon upon plates taken from the plains of Nephi, wherefore it is an abridgement of the record of the people of Nephi, and also of the Lamanites, written to the Lamanites, which are a remnant of the House of Israel, and also to Jew and Gentile. Written by way of commandment, and also by the spirit of prophecy and of Revelation.'—'By Joseph Smith, Junior, Author and proprietor. From plates dug out of the earth, in the township of Manchester, Ontario, New York.—Palmyra, printed by E.B. Grandin, for the Author, 1830. It is a collection of books said to have been written by different persons during the interval of 1020 years—the 1st and second books of Nephi occupy 122 pages; the Book of Jacob the brother of Nephi occupies 21; that of Enos 3; that of Jarom 2; that of Omin 4; the words of Mormon 3; the book of Mosiah 68; that of Alma 186; that of Helaman 44; that of Nephi the son of Helaman 66; that of Mormon 20; that of Ether 35; and that of Morom 14 pages; making in all 588 octavo pages.

This romance—but this is for it a name too innocent—begins with the religious adventures of one Lehi, whose wife was Sariah, and their four sons, Laman, Lemuel, Sam, and Nephi. Lehi lived in Jerusalem all his life, up to the first year of Zedekiah, King of Judah, and when the prophets appeared foretelling the utter destruction of Jerusalem, Lehi humbled himself, and after various visions and revelations, started with his sons into the wilderness. Lehi, before his departure, forgot to bring with him the records of his family, and that of the Jews; but Nephi, his younger son, with much pious courage returned and succeeded in getting upon plates of brass the records of the Jews from the creation down to the first year of Zedekiah, King of Judah, and also the prophets including many prophecies delivered by Jeremiah.

From the records it appeared that this Lehi was a son of Joseph. He prevailed on one Ishmael and his family to accompany him into the wilderness, whose daughters the sons of Lehi took for wives.

Lehi was a greater prophet than any of the Jewish prophets, and uttered all the events of the Christian era, and developed the records of Matthew, Luke, and John, six hundred years before John the Baptist was born.—These pilgrims travelled several days journey in some wilderness, 'a south, south-east direction, along the borders of the Red Sea.' A ball with pointers on it, inscribed with various intelligence, legible at proper times, was the pillar and index in passing through the wilderness for many, very many days. By their bow and arrow they lived for eight years, travelling an easterly course from Jerusalem, until they came to a great sea. By divine revelation Nephi constructed a ship, and although opposed by his unbelieving brethren, being greatly assisted by the Holy Spirit, he succeeded in launching her safely, and got all his tribe, with all their stock of seeds, animals, and provisions, safely aboard. They had 'a compass' which none but Nephi knew how to manage; but the Lord had promised them a fine land, and after many perils and trials, and a long passage, they safely arrived in the land of promise. Nephi made brazen plates soon after his arrival in America, for that was the land of promise to them, and on these plates be marked their peregrinations and adventures, and all the prophecies which God gave to him concerning the future destinies of his people, and the human race.

After his father's death, his brethren rebelled against him. They finally separated in the wilderness, and became the heads of different tribes, often in the lapse of generations making incurations upon each other. The Nephites, like their father, for many generations were good Christians, believers in the doctrines of the Calvinists and Methodists, and preaching baptism and other Christian usages hundreds of years before Jesus Christ was born!

Before Nephi died, which was about fifty-five years from the flight of Lehi from Jerusalem, he had preached to his people everything which is now preached in the state of New York, and anointed or ordained his brother Enos 'in the nurture and admonition of the Lord,' gave him the plates, and left him successor in office over the people of Nephi. Enos says 'there came a voice to me, saying, Enos thy sins are forgiven thee, and thou shalt be blessed. And, I sayeth, Lord how it is done. And he sayeth unto me, Because of thy faith in Christ, whom thou hast not heard nor seen.' p. 143. Enos died one hundred seventy-nine years from the hegira of Lehi; consequently, this happened four hundred thirty-one years before Jesus Christ was born. He was a contemporary with Nehemiah, and may we not say how much wiser and more enlightened were the Nephites in America than the Jews at their return to Jerusalem!

Enos gave the plates to Jarom, his son. In his time 'they kept the law of Moses and the Sabbath day holy to the Lord.' During the priesthood and reign of Enos, there were many commotions and wars between his people and the Lamanites. Then the sharp pointed arrow, the quiver, and the dart were invented. Jarom delivered his plates to his son Omni, and gave up the ghost two hundred thirty-eight years from the flight of Lehi. Omni died two hundred seventy-six from the hegira, and gave the plates to his son Amaron, who in the year three hundred and twenty, gave them to his brother Chemish; he, to his son Abinadom; he to his son Amaleki; and he having no son, gave them to the just and pious King Benjamin. King Benjamin had three sons, Mosiah, Helorum, and Helaman, whom he educated in all the learning of his fathers. To Mosiah he delivered up the plates of Nephi, the ball which guided them through the wilderness, and the sword of one Laban, of mighty renown. King Benjamin addressed his people from the new temple which they had erected, for they had, even then, built a temple, synagogues, and a tower, in the New World.

King Benjamin assembled the people to sacrifice according to the law around the new temple; and he enjoined upon them, at the same time, the Christian institutions, and gave them a Patriarchal valedictory. After they had heard him speak, and had offered up their sacrifices, they fell down and prayed in the following words: 'O have mercy, and apply the atoning blood of Christ, that we may receive forgiveness of our sins, and our hearts may be purified; for we believe in Jesus Christ the son of God, who created heaven and earth and all things, who shall come down upon the children of men.' Then the spirit of the Lord fell upon them and they were filled with joy, having received a remission of their sins.' p. 162.

King Benjamin ordered his people to take upon them the name of Christ, and in these remarkable words,—'There is no other name given whereby salvation cometh; therefore I would that you should take upon you the name of Christ, all you that have entered into the covenant with God that ye should be obedient unto the end of your lives.—page 166. They all took upon them the name of Christ, and he having ordained them priests and teachers, and appointed his son, Mosiah, to reign in his stead, gave up the Ghost 476 years after Lehi's escape from Jerusalem, and one hundred twenty-four before Christ was born, Mosiah gave up the plates of brass, and all the things which we had kept, to Alma the son of Alma, who was appointed 'chief judge and high priest,' the people willing to have no king, and Mosiah died five hundred sixty-nine years from the time Lehi left Jerusalem.

In the 14th year of the Judges, and 69 years before the birth of Jesus, they sent out missionary priests, who preached through all the tribes of the country against all vices, holding 'forth the coming of the soul of God, his sufferings, death and resurrection, and that he should appear unto them after his resurrection: and this the people did hear with great joy and gladness.'—p. 268.

Alma's book reaches down to the end of the 39th year of the Judges. These were wonderful years—many cities were founded, many battles were fought, fortifications reared, letters written, and even in one year a certain Hagoth built an exceeding large ship, and launched it forth into the west sea. in this embarked many of the Nephites. This same ship-builder the next year built other ships, one was lost with all its passengers and crew.—p.406.

Many prophecies were pronounced; one that in 400 years after the coming of Christ, the Nephites would lose their religion. During the time of the Judges, many were called Christians by name, and 'baptism unto repentance' was a common thing. 'And it came to pass that they did appoint priests and teachers through all the land, and over all the churches.'—p.349. 'And those who did belong to the church were faithful, yea all those who were true believers in Christ took upon them gladly the name of Christ, or Christians, as they were called, because of their belief in Christ.'—Page 301. 'And it came to pass that there were many who died firmly believing that their souls were redeemed by the Lord Jesus Christ: thus they went out of the world rejoicing.'—p. 353. The word was preached by Helaman, Shiblon, Corianton, Amnon, and his brethren, etc. yea and all those, who had been ordained by the holy order of God, being baptized unto repentance, and sent forth to preach unto the people.' Page 623. This happened in the nineteenth year of the Judges, seventy-two years before the birth of Jesus. Before this time synagogues with pulpits were built, 'for the Zoramites,' a sort of Episcopalians, 'gathered themselves together on one day of the week, which day they called the day of the Lord.'—'And they had a place which was high and lifted up, which held but one man, who read prayers, the same prayers every week; and this high place was called Rameumpton, which being interpreted, is the holy stand.'—p.311. The book of Helaman reacheth down to the ninetieth year of the Judges, and to the year preceding that in which the Messiah was born. During the period embraced in Helaman's narrative, many ten thousands were baptized. 'And behold the holy spirit of God did come down from heaven, and did enter into their hearts, and they were filled as with fire, and they could speak forth marvelous words.'—p. 421.

Masonry was invented about this time; for men began to bind themselves in secret oaths to aid one another in all things, good or evil.—p.424. Powers of loosing and binding in heaven were conferred upon Nephi, the son of Helaman, and all miraculous power, such as the apostles possessed. One Samuel, also foretold that 'the Christ would be born in five years, and that the night before should be as light as day; and that the day of his death should be a day of darkness like the night.'—p.445. The book of this Nephi commences with the birth of the Messiah, six hundred years from the departure of Lehi from Jerusalem. In the midst of the threats of the infidels to slaughter the faithful, the sun set; but lo! the night was clear as mid-day, and from that period they changed their era, and counted time as we do. A star also appeared, but it is not stated how it could be seen in a night as bright as day; but it was universally seen throughout all the land, to the salvation of the pious from the threats of their enemies. The terrors of the day of his death are also stated, and in the thirty-fourth year from his nativity, after his resurrection, he descended from heaven and visited the people of Nephi. Jesus called upon them to examine his hands and his sides, as he did Thomas, though none of them had expressed a doubt. Two thousand five hundred men, women and children, one by one, examined him, and then worshipped him. He commanded Nephi to baptize, and gave him the words which he was to use, viz: 'Having authority given me, of Jesus Christ, I baptize you in the name of the Father and of the Son, and of the Holy Ghost. Amen.' He commissioned eleven others, who with Nephi, were his twelve American Apostles, and promised himself to baptize their converts 'with fire and with the Holy Spirit.'

He delivers them the sermon upon the mount, and some other sayings recorded in Matthew, Mark, Luke, and John; He healed all their diseases, and prayed for their children; but the things spoken were so great and marvelous that they could not be spoken nor written.

He ordained one to administer the supper, who alone had authority to dispense it to the disciples baptized in his name. The only new commandments which were given to the American Christians on his occasional visits which were repeated, were—'Pray in your families unto the Father, always in my name, that your wives and your children may be blessed.' 'Meet often, and forbid no man from coming unto you when you shall meet together.'—p. 492.

Nephi was chief among the twelve apostles: he baptized himself, and then baptized the eleven, whose names were Timothy, Jonas, Mathoni and Mathoninah, Kumen, Kumenonhi, Jeremiah, Shimnon, Jonas, Zedekiah, and Isaiah, They were baptized in fire and the Holy Ghost.' Not a new word, however, should be written in addition to those found in the New Testament; for although he spake for several days to these American disciples, none of the new and marvelous sayings could be uttered or written! He inspected the plates of Nephi, and only found one omission, which was that he failed to mention the resurrection of many saints in America at the time of the tempest and earthquake. He commanded these Nephites to be called Christians.

The book of Nephi the son of Nephi, gives, in four pages, the history of 320 years after Christ. In the thirty-sixth year, all the inhabitants of the land were converted; there was a perfect community and no disputations in the land for one hundred seventy years. Three of the American apostles were never to die, and were seen four hundred years after Christ; but what has become of them no one can tell, except Cowdery, Whitmer and Harris, the three witnesses of the truth of the plates of Nephi, be these three immortal men. Towards the close of the history of Nephi or the record Ammaron, sects and divisions and battles became frequent, and all goodness had almost left the continent in the year three hundred and twenty.

Mormon appears next in the drama, the recording angel of the whole matter, who, by the way, was a mighty general and great Christian; he commanded in one engagement forty-two thousand men against the Lamanites!!! He was no Quaker! This dreadful battle was fought A.D. 330. The Lamanites took South America for themselves, and gave North America to the Nephites. Mormon was very orthodox, for he preached in these words, A.D. 362:—'That Jesus was the very Christ and the very God.' He must have heard of the Arian controversy by some angel!!

Moroni finishes what Mormon his father, left undone, and continues the history, till A.D. 400. He pleads that no one shall disbelieve his record because of its imperfections!! and declares that none who receive it will condemn it on account of its imperfections, and for not doing so, the same shall know greater things. p.—532. 'He that condemneth it shall be in danger of hell fire.' He laments the prevalence of free masonry in the times when his book should be dug up out of the earth, and proves that miracles will never cease; because God is the same yesterday, to day, and forever—consequently must always create suns, moons, and stars, every day!! He exhorted to 'take heed that none be baptized without telling their experience, nor partake of the sacrament of Christ unworthily?!!—p.537. Moroni, in the conclusion of his book of Mormon, says if his plates had been larger we should have written in Hebrew; but because of this difficulty he wrote in the 'Reformed Egyptian,' being handed down and altered unto us according to our manner of speech.—p.538. 'Condemn me not,' says he, 'because of mine imperfections; neither my father, because of his imperfections, neither them which have written before him; but rather give thanks unto God that he hath made manifest unto you our imperfections, that you may learn to be more wise than we have been.'—p.538. A very necessary advice, indeed!!

Moroni writes the book of Ether, containing an account of the people of Jared, who escaped from the building of the tower of Babel unconfounded in his language. These people of Jared, God marched before in a cloud, and directed them through the wilderness, and instructed them to build barges to cross seas; and finally they built eight barges, air tight, and were commanded to make a hole in the top to admit air, and one in the bottom to admit water, and in them were put sixteen windows of molten stone, which when touched by the finger of Jesus, became as transparent as glass, and gave them light under 'the mountain waves,' and when above the water. He that touched these stones, appeared unto the brother of Jared, and said, behold I am Jesus Christ, I am the father and the son.' Two of these stones were sealed up with the plates and became the spectacles of Joseph Smith, according to a prediction uttered before Abraham was born. It was also foretold in the book of Ether, written by Moroni, that he that should find the plates should have the privilege of showing the plates unto those who shall assist to bring forth this work, and unto three shall they be shown by the power of God: wherefore they shall of a surety known that these things are true.—p.548.

And the 8 barges, air-tight, made like ducks, after swimming and diving 334 days, arrived on the coasts of the land of promise. The book of Ether relates the wars and carnage amongst these people. In the lapse of generations, they counted two millions of mighty men, besides women and children, slain; and finally, they were all killed but one, and he fell to the earth as if he had no life. So ends the book of Ether. -p.573.

The book of Moroni details the manner of ordaining priests and teachers, the manner of administering ordinances, and the epistles of Mormon to his soon Moroni. Moroni seal up the record A.D. 420, and assures the world that spiritual gifts shall never cease, only through unbelief. And when the plates of Nephi should be dug out of the earth, he declares that men should ask God the Eternal Father, in the name of Christ, 'If these things were not true.' 'If with a sincere heart and real intent, having faith in Christ, such prayers are made, ye shall know the truth of all things.' -p.586. The testimony of Oliver Cowdery, David Whitmer, and Martin Harris, asserting that they saw the plates, is appended. They also testify that they know that they have been translated by the gift and power of God, for his voice has declared it unto them.

Another testimony is appended signed by four Whitmers, one Hiram Page, and three Smiths, affirming that they saw the plates, handled them, and that Smith has got the plates in his possession.

Such is an analysis of the book of Mormon, the bible of the Mormonites. For noticing of which I would have asked forgiveness from all my readers, had not several hundred persons of different denominations believed in it. On this account alone has it become necessary to notice it, and for the same reason we must examine its pretensions to divine authority; for it purports to be a revelation from God. And in the first place, we shall examine its internal evidences.

Internal Evidences

It admits the Old and New Testaments to contain the revelations, institutions and commandments of God to Patriarchs, Jews, and Gentiles, down to the year 1830, and always, as such, speaks of them and quotes them. This admission at once blasts its pretensions to credibility. Admitting the bible now received to have come from God, it is impossible that the book of Mormon came from the same author. For the following reasons: -

1. Smith, its real author, as ignorant and impudent a knave as ever wrote a book, betrays the cloven foot in basing his whole book upon a false fact, or a pretended fact, which makes God a liar. It is this:—With the Jews, God made a covenant at Mount Sinai, and instituted a priesthood and a high priesthood. The priesthood he gave to the tribe of Levi, and the high priesthood to Aaron and his sons for an everlasting priesthood. He separated Levi, and covenanted to give him this office irrevocably while ever the temple stood, or till the Messiah came. 'Then, says God Moses shall appoint Aaron and his sons, and they shall wait on their priest's office, and the stranger, (the person of another family,) who cometh nigh, shall be put to death.' Numbers 3:10. 'And the priests, the sons of Levi, shall come near; for them the Lord thy God hath chosen to minister unto him, and to bless in the name of the Lord, and by their word shall every controversy and every stroke be tried.' Deut. 21:5. Korah, Dathan, and Abiram, with 250 men of renown, rebelled against a part of the institution of the priesthood, and the Lord destroyed them in the presence of the whole congregation. This was to be a memorial that no stranger invade any part of the office of the priesthood. Num. 16:40. Fourteen thousand and seven hundred of the people were destroyed by a plague for murmuring against this memorial.

In the 18th chapter of Numbers the Levites are again given to Aaron and his sons, and the priesthood confirmed to them with this threat—'The stranger that cometh night shall be put to death.' 'Even Jesus, says Paul, were he on earth, could not be a priest, for he was of a tribe concerning which Moses spake nothing of priesthood.' Heb. 7:13. So irrevocable was the grant of the priesthood to Levi, and of the high priesthood to Aaron, that no stranger dare approach the altar of God which Moses established. Hence, Jesus himself was excluded from officiating as priest on earth according to the law.

This Joseph Smith overlooked in his impious fraud, and makes his hero Lehi spring from Joseph. And just as soon as his sons return with the roll of his lineage, ascertaining that he was of the tribe of Joseph, he and his sons acceptably 'offer sacrifices and burnt offerings to the Lord.'—p.15. Also it is repeated, p. 18—Nephi became chief artificer, ship-builder and mariner; was scribe, prophet, priest and king unto his own people, and 'consecrated Jacob and Joseph, the sons of his father, priests to God and teachers—almost six hundred years before the fullness of the times of the Jewish economy was completed. p.72. Nephi represents himself withal as 'under the law of Moses,' p. 105. They build a temple in the new world, and in 55 years after they leave Jerusalem, make a new priesthood which God approbates. A high priest is also consecrated, and yet they are all the while 'teaching the law of Moses, and exhorting the people to keep it!—p.146,209. Thus God is represented as instituting, approbating and blessing a new priesthood from the tribe of Joseph, concerning which Moses gave no commandment concerning priesthood. Although God had promised in the law of Moses, that if any man, not of the tribe and family of Levi and Aaron, should approach the office of priest, he would surely die; he is represented by Smith as blessing, approbating, and sustaining another family in this approbated office. The God of Abraham or Joseph Smith must then be a liar!! And who will hesitate to pronounce him an imposter? This lie runs through his records for the first six hundred years' of his story.

2. This ignorant and impudent liar, in the next place, makes the God of Abraham, Isaac and Jacob, violate his covenants with Israel and Judah, concerning the land of Canaan, by promising a new land to the pious Jew.

If a company of reprobate Jews had departed from Jerusalem and the temple, in the days of Zedekiah, and founded a new colony, it would not have been so incongruous. But to represent God as inspiring a devout Jew and a prophet, such as Levi and Nephi are represented by Smith, with a resolution to forsake Jerusalem and God's own house, and to depart from the land which God swore to their fathers so long as they were obedient; and to guide by a miracle and to bless by prodigies a good man in forsaking God's covenant and worship—is so monstrous an error, that language fails to afford a name for it. It is to make God violate his own covenants, and set at naught his own promises, and to convert his own curses into blessings. Excision from the commonwealth of Israel, and banishment from Jerusalem and the temple, were the greatest curses the law of Moses knew. But Smith makes a good and pious Jew the subject of this curse, and sends him off into the inhospitable wilderness, disinherits him in Canaan, and makes him more happy in forsaking the institutions of Moses, more intelligent in the wilderness, and more prosperous in adversity, than even the Jews in their best days, in the best of lands, and under the best of all governments!!! The imposter was too ignorant of the history of the Jews and the nature of the covenants of promise, to have even alluded to them in his book, if he had not supposed that he had the plates of Moses in his own keeping, as he had his 'molten plates' of Nephi. To separate a family from the nation of Israel, was to accumulate all the curses of the law upon that family.—Deut. 29:21.

3. He has more of the Jews, living in the new world, than could have been numbered anywhere else, even in the days of John the Baptist; and has placed them under a new dynasty. The scepter, with

him, has departed from Judah, and a lawgiver from among his descendants, hundreds of years before Shiloh came; and king Benjamin is a wiser and more renowned king than king Solomon. He seems to have gone upon an adage which saith, 'the more marvelous, the more credible the tale,' and the less of fact, and the more of fiction, the more intelligible and reasonable the narrative.

4. He represents the temple worship as continued in his new land of promise contrary to every precept of the law, and so happy are the people of Nephi as never to shed a tear on account of the excision, nor turn an eye toward Jerusalem or God's temple. The pious Jews in their captivity turned their faces to Jerusalem and the holy place, and remembered God's promises concerning the place where he recorded his name. They hung their harps upon the willow, and could not sing the songs of Zion in a foreign land; but the Nephites have not a single wish for Jerusalem, for they can, in their wigwam temple, in the wilderness of America, enjoy more of God's presence than the most righteous Jew could enjoy in that house of which David had rather be a doorkeeper, than to dwell in the tabernacles of men. And all this too, when God's only house of prayer, according to his covenant with Israel, stood in Jerusalem.

5. ***Malachi, the last of the Jewish prophets, commanded Israel to regard the law of Moses till the Messiah came***. And Moses commanded them to regard him till the Great Prophet came. But Nephi and Smith's prophets institute ordinances and observances for the Jews, subversive of Moses, 500 years before the Great Prophet came.

6. ***Passing over a hundred similar errors, we shall next notice his ignorance of the New Testament matters and things***. The twelve Apostles of the Lamb, are said by Paul, to have developed certain secrets, which were hid for ages and generations, which Paul says were ordained before the world to their glory, that they should have the honor of announcing them. But Smith makes his pious hero

Nephi, 600 years before the Messiah began to preach, and disclose these secrets concerning the calling of the Gentiles, and the blessings flowing through the Messiah to Jews and Gentiles, which Paul says were hid for ages and generations, 'which in these ages was not made known unto the sons of men, as it is now revealed unto us the holy Apostles and prophets, by the spirit; that the Gentiles should be fellow heirs and of the same body and partakers of his promise in Christ by the Gospel.' Smith makes Nephi express every truth found in the writings of the Apostles concerning the calling and blessing of the Gentiles, and even quotes the 11th chapter of Romans, and many other passages before he had a son grown in the wilderness able to aim an arrow at a deer. Paul says these things were secrets and unknown until his time; but Smith makes Nephi say the same things 600 years before Paul was converted! One of the two is a false prophet. Mormonites, take your choice!

7. This prophet Smith, through his stone spectacles, wrote on the plates of Nephi, in his book of Mormon, every error and almost every truth discussed in N. York for the last ten years. He decides all the great controversies—infant baptism, ordination, the trinity, regeneration, repentance, justification, the fall of man, the atonement, transubstantiation, fasting, penance, church government, religious experience, the call to the ministry, the general resurrection, eternal punishment, who may baptize, and even the question of freemasonry, republican government, and the rights of man. All these topics are repeatedly alluded to. How much more benevolent and intelligent this American Apostle, than were the holy twelve, and Paul to assist them!!! He prophesied of all these topics, and of the apostasy, and infallibly decided, by his authority, every question. How easy to prophecy of the past or of the present time!!

8. But he is better skilled in the controversies in New York than in the geography or history of Judea. He makes John baptize in the village of Bethabara, (page 22) and says Jesus was born in Jerusalem, p. 240. Great must be the faith of the Mormonites in this new Bible!!! The mariners compass was only known in Europe about 300 years ago; but Nephi knew all about steam boats and the compass 2400 years ago.

9. He represents the Christian institution as practiced among his Israelites before Jesus was born.

And his Jews are called Christians while keeping the law of Moses, the holy Sabbath, and worshipping in their temple at their altars, and by their high priests.

10. But not to honor him by a too minute examination and exposition, I will sum up the whole of the internal evidence which I deem worthy of remark, in the following details: -

The book professes to be written at intervals and by different persons during the long period of 1020 years. And yet for uniformity of style, there never was a book more evidently written by one set of fingers, nor more certainly conceived in one cranium since the first book appeared in human language, than this same book. If I could swear to any man's voice, face or person, assuming different names, I could swear that this book was written by one man. And as Joseph Smith is a very ignorant man and is called the author on the title page, I cannot doubt for a single moment that he is the sole author and proprietor of it. As a specimen of his style the reader will take the following samples—Page 4th. In his own preface:—'The plates of which hath been spoken.' In the last page, 'the plates of which hath been spoken.' In the certificate signed by Cowdery and his two witnesses, he has the same idiom, 'which came from the tower of which hath been spoken;' page 16, 'we are a descendant of Joseph.' 'The virgin which thou seest is the mother of God.' 'Behold the Lamb of God the Eternal Father,' p. 25; 'Ye are like unto they,' 'and I saith unto them,' p.44. 'We did arrive to the promised land;' p.49, 'made mention upon the first plate,' p.50.

Nephi 2400 years ago hears the saying of a Pagan who lived 634 years after him—'The God of nature suffers.' p.51. 'The righteous need not fear, for it is they which shall not be confounded.' p.58. Shakespeare was read by Nephi 2200 years before he was born—'The silent grave from whence no traveller returns,' 61. 'Your own eternal welfare' was a phrase then common in America, p.62. 'Salvation is free' was then announced. 'That Jesus should rise from the dead' was repeatedly declared on this continent in the reign of Nebuchadnezzar. And at the same time it was said, 'Messiah cometh in the fullness of time that he might redeem the children of men from the fall;' p.65. 'The fall' was frequently spoken of at the Isthmus of Darien 2400 years ago.

I had no object, says Nephi, in the reign of Zedekiah, 'but the everlasting salvation of your souls.' 66. 'I had spake many things,' 'for a more history part are written upon mine other plates.' 69. 'Do not anger again because of mine enemies,' p. 70. 'For it behoveth the Great Creator that he die for all men.' 'It must needs be an infinite atonement.' 'This flesh must go to its mother earth.' 'And this death must deliver up its dead,' p.70, were common phrases 2300 years ago—'for the atonement satisfieth the demands of his justice upon all those who have not the law given them,' p. 81. The Calvinists were in America before Nephi. 'The Lord remembereth all they,' 85. The atonement is infinite for all mankind,' p.104. The Americans knew this on the Columbo 2400 years ago. 'His name shall be called Jesus Christ the Son of God.' An angel told this to Nephi 545 years before it was told to Mary, p.105. 'And they shall teach with their learning and deny the Holy Ghost which giveth them utterance;' this prophecy was at that time delivered against us, p.112. 'My words shall hiss forth unto the ends of the earth,' p.115. 'Wherein did the Lamb of God fill all the righteousness in being baptized by water,' 118. This question was discussed 2300 years ago. 'The baptism by fire and the Holy Ghost was preached in the days of Cyrus,' p.119. 'The only true doctrine of the Father and of the Son and of the Holy Ghost which is one God without end. Amen,' p.120. This was decided in the time of Daniel the Prophet. 'I glory in plainness,' says Nephi. 'Christ will show you that these are his words in the last day,' p.122. Too late to prove your mission, Mr. Nephi!

'After that ye have obtained a hope in Christ, ye shall obtain riches if you seek them.' So spoke Jacob in the days of Ezekiel the Prophet. 'They believed in Christ and worshipped the Father in his name,' p.129. This was said by Jacob in the time of Daniel. 'Do as ye hath hitherto done,' says Mosiah, page 158. These Smith-isms are in every page. 'And his mother shall be called Mary.' p.160. 'The Son of God and Father of heaven and earth.' p.161. 'The infant perisheth not, that dieth in his infancy.' 'For the natural man is an enemy of God and was from the fall of Adam, and will be forever and ever,' p.161. This was spoken by King Benjamin 124 years before Christ. He was a Yankee, too, for he spoke like Smith, saying, 'I who ye call your king.' 'They saith unto the king,' p.182. This was another Joseph Smith called Mosiah. 'They were baptized in the waters of Mormon, and were called the church of Christ,' p.192. This happened 100 years before Christ was born. 'Alma, why persecuteth thou the church of God,' p.222. 'Ye must be born again; yea, born of God—changed from their carnal and fallen state to a state of righteousness,' 214. This was preached also 100 years before Christ was born. 'These things had not ought to be,' 220.

'I, Alma, being consecrated by my father Alma to be a high priest over the church of God, he having power and authority from God to do these things (p. 232) say unto you, except ye repent ye can in no wise enter into the Kingdom of Heaven.' 237. 'He ordained priests and elders, by laying on his hands, to watch over the church'—'Not so much as a hair of the head shall be lost in the grave'—'The holy order of the high priesthood.' p.250. The high priesthood of Alma was about 80 years before Christ. 'The Lord poured out his spirit to prepare the minds of the people for the preaching of Alma, preaching repentance.' p.268. Alma was a Yankee of Smith's school, for he saith: 'The light of everlasting light was lit up in his soul.' p.47.

During the pontificate of Alma men prayed thus: 'If there is a God, and if thou art God wilt thou make thyself known unto me.' p.286. Alma 'clapped his hands upon all they which were with him.' p.313. 'Instruments in the hand of God' were the preachers of Alma. p.323. Modest and orthodox men, truly! 'If ye deny the Holy Ghost when it once hath place in you, and ye know that ye deny, behold this is the unpardonable sin.' p.332. So Alma preached. 'And now my son, ye are called of God to preach the Gospel.' p.340. 'They were high priests over the church.' p.350. 'The twenty and second year of the Judges this came to pass.' p.364. 'They were valiant for courage.' p.376.

These are but as one drop out of a bucket compared with the amount of Smith-isms in this book. It is patched up and cemented with 'And it came to pass'—'I sayeth unto you'—'Ye saith unto him'—and all the King James' HATHS, DIDS and DOTHS—in the lowest imitation of the common version; and is, without exaggeration, the meanest book in the English language; but it is a translation made through stone spectacles, in a dark room, and in the hat of the prophet Smith from the REFORMED EGYPTIAN!! It has not one good sentence in it, save the profanation of those sentences quoted from the Oracles of the living God. I would as soon compare a bat to the American eagle, a mouse to a mammoth, or the deformities of a specter to the beauties of Him whom John saw in Patmos, as to contrast it with a single chapter in all the writings of the Jewish or Christian prophets. It is as certainly Smith's fabrication as Satan is the father of lies, or darkness the offspring of night. So much for the internal evidences of the Book of Mormon.

Its external evidences are, first, the testimony of the prophets Cowdery, Whitmer, and Harris; who saw the plates and heard the voice of God; who are disinterested retailers of the books. I would ask them how they knew that it was God's voice which they heard—but they would tell me to ask God in faith. THAT IS, I MUST BELIEVE IT FIRST, AND THEN ASK GOD IF IT BE TRUE! 'Tis better to take Nephi's proof which is promised to us in the day of final judgment! They say that spiritual gifts are continued to the end of time among the true believers. They are true believers—have they wrought any miracles? They have tried, but their faith failed. Can they show any spiritual gift? Yes, they can mutter Indian and traffic in new Bibles.

'But Smith is the wonder of the world.' So was the Apocalyptic beast!

'an ignorant young man.' That needs no proof. Gulliver's Travels is a heroic problem in comparison of this book of Smith.

'But he cannot write a page.' Neither could Mahomet, who gave forth the Alcoran.

'Smith is an honest looking fellow.' So was Simon Magus, the sorcerer.

'But he was inspired.' So was Judas, by Satan.

Its external evidences are also the subscriptions of four Whitmers, three Smiths, and one Page, the relatives and connections of Joseph Smith, junior. And these 'men handled as many of the brazen or golden leaves as the said Smith translated.' So did I. But Smith has got the plates of which hath been spoken. Let him show them. Their certificate proves nothing, save that Smith wrote it, and they signed it. But Smith gives testimony himself. There is one who says, 'If I bear testimony of myself, my testimony ought not to be regarded.'

If this prophet and his three prophetic witnesses had aught of speciosity about them or their book, we would have examined it and exposed it in a different manner. I have never felt myself so fully authorized to address mortal man in the style in which Paul addressed Elymas the sorcerer as I feel towards this Atheist Smith. His three witnesses, I am credibly informed, on one of their horse- swapping and prophetic excursions in the Sandusky country, having bartered horses three times for once preaching, represented Walter Scott and myself as employed in translating these plates, and as believers in the book of Mormon. If there was anything plausible about Smith, I would say to those who believe him to be a prophet, hear the question which Moses put into the mouth of the Jews, and his answer to it—'And if thou say in thine heart, HOW SHALL WE KNOW THE WORD WHICH THE LORD HATH NOT SPOKEN?'—Does he answer, 'ASK THE LORD AND HE WILL TELL YOU?'—Does he say 'Wait till the day of judgment and you will know?' Nay, indeed; but—'When a prophet speaketh in the name of the Lord, if the thing follow not nor come to pass, that is the thing which the Lord hath not spoken; the prophet hath spoken it presumptuously: THOU SHALT NOT BE AFRAID OF HIM.' Deuteronomy 18:8. Smith has failed in every instance to verify one of his own sayings.

Again, I would say in the words of the Lord by Isaiah, 'Bring forth your strong reasons, saith the King of Jacob: let them bring them forth and show us what shall happen: let them show the former things what they mean, that we may consider them, and know the latter end of them—show the things which are to come hereafter, that we may know that you are prophets: yea, do good or do evil, that we may be dismayed and behold it together. Behold you are nothing, and your work of naught: an abomination is every one that chooseth you.' Isaiah 41:21- 23.

Let the children of Mormon ponder well, if yet reason remains with them, the following passage from Isaiah 44; and if they cannot see the analogy between themselves and the sons of ancient imposture, then reason is of as little use to them as it was to those of whom the prophet spake—

'The carpenters having chosen a piece of wood framed it by rule and glued the parts together, and made it in the form of a man, and with the comeliness of a man, to set it in a house. He cut wood from the forest which the Lord planted—a pine tree, which the rain had nourished, that it might be fuel for the use of man: and having taken some of it he warmed himself; and with other pieces they made a fire and baked cakes, and of the residue they made gods and worshipped them. Did he not burn half of it in the fire, and, with the coals of that half bake cakes: and having roasted meat with it did he not eat and was satisfied; and when warmed say, "Aha! I am warmed, I have enjoyed the fire?" Yet of the residue he made a carved god, and worshipped it, and prayeth to it, saying, "Deliver me, for thou art my God."

'They had not sense to think; for they were so involved in darkness that they could not see with their eyes, nor understand with their hearts: nor did any reason in his mind, nor by his understanding recollect, that he had burned half of it in the fire, and on the coals thereof baked cakes, and had roasted flesh and eaten, and of the residue had made an abomination; so they bow themselves down to it. Know thou that their heart is ashes, and they are led astray and none can deliver his soul. Take a view of it, will you not say, "There is indeed a lie in my right hand?"

'Remember these things, O Jacob, even thou Israel, for thou art my servant. I have made thee my servant; therefore O Israel do not thou forget me. For, lo! I have made thy transgressions vanish like a cloud—and thy sins like the murky vapor. Return to me, and I will redeem thee.'

A. CAMPBELL. February 10, 1831.

DEMONOLOGY

By Alexander Campbell

Demonology

An address delivered to the Popular Lecture Club, Nashville, Tennessee, March 10, 1841.

Mr. President, and gentlemen members of the popular lecture club,

While the antiquary is gathering up the moldering ruins of ancient temples, palaces, and cities; or poring over the coins, medals, and statues of other ages, seeking to prove or to embellish some theory of the olden times: while the astronomer is directing his largest telescope to some remote ethereal field, far beyond the milky way, in search of new nebula, unseen before, in hope to find the nucleus of some incipient solar system: while the speculative geologist is delving down to the foundations of the eternal mountains, in quest of new evidences of his doctrine of successive and long protracted formations of the massy strata of Mother Earth, "rock-ribbed and ancient as the Sun:" while the skeptic is exultingly scanning the metaphysical dreams of some imaginary system of Nature, or seeking in the desolations of the ancient Mythologies arguments against the mighty facts and overwhelming demonstrations of the Christian faith—may I be indulged, gentlemen, to invite you into the precincts of Demonology, and to accompany me in a brief excursion into the land of demons, whence, dark and mysterious though it be, we may, perhaps, guided by some friendly star, elicit some useful light on that grand and awful world of spirits, which, as we descend the hill of life, rises higher and higher in its demands upon our time and thoughts, as embracing the all-absorbing and transcendent interests of human kind.

Think not, however, that I intend to visit the fairy realms and enchanting scenes of wild romance; or that I wish to indulge in the fascinating fictions of poets, ancient or modern; think not that I am about to ascend with old Hesiod into his curious theogony of gods and demigods, or to descend with our late Sir Walter Scott to the phantasmatic realms of his Celtic and Scottish ghosts and demons. I aim at more substantial entertainment, at more sober and grave realities, than the splendid fancies of those gifted and fortunate votaries of popular applause, rather than of the approvals of the conscientious and sedate.

It is the subject of demons, as forming a portion of the real antiquities of the world—as connected with Pagan, Jewish, and Christian theology;—it is the subject of demons, sometimes called devils, not in their fictitious, but true character, that I propose to discuss: for even here there is the fact and the fable, the true and the false, the real and the imaginary, as in everything else. The extravagant fancies of the poets, the ghosts and specters of the dark ages, have spread their sable mantles upon this subject, and involved it all either in philosophical dubiety, or in a blind indiscriminate infidelity.

The inductive and Christian philosopher in this department, as in most others, finds both truth and fable blended in the same tradition; and, therefore, neither awed by authority, nor allured by the fascinations of novelty, he institutes an examination into the merits of a subject, which, if true, cannot but deeply interest the thoughtful; and which, if false, should be banished from the minds of all.

That a class of beings of some sort, designated *demons,* has been an element of the faith, an object of the dread and veneration of all ages and nations, as far back as all memory reaches, no one who believes in a spiritual system—no one who regards the volumes of divine inspiration, or who is only partially acquainted with Pagan and Jewish antiquity, can reasonably doubt. But concerning these demons, of what order of intelligences, of what character and destiny; of what powers intellectual and moral, or immoral, there has been much debate, and still there is need of farther and more satisfactory examination.

Before entering either philosophically or practically into this investigation, it is necessary that we define the true and proper meaning of the term *demon.* This word, it is said, is of Grecian origin and character—of which, however, we have not full assurance. In that language it is written and pronounced *daimoon;* and, according to some etymologists, is legitimately descended from a very ancient verb pronounced *daioo,* which means *to discriminate, to know. Daimoon,* or *demon,* therefore, simply indicates a person of intelligence—*a knowing one.* Thus before the age of philosophy, or the invention of the name, those were called demons, as a title of honor, who afterwards assumed the more modest title of philosophers. Aristotle, for his great learning was called *demon,* as was the celebrated Thucydides: hence among the Platonists it was for some time a title of honor. But this, it must be observed, was a special appropriation, like our use of the words *divine* and *reverend.* When we apply these titles to sinful men, who, because of their calling, ought to be not only intelligent, but of a divine and celestial temper and morality, we use them by a special indulgence from that sovereign pontiff with whom is the *jus et norma loquendi.*

But as some of the Platonists elevated the spirits of departed heroes, public benefactors, and distinguished men, into a species of demigods or mediators between them and the Supreme Divinity, as some of our forefathers were accustomed to regard the souls of departed saints, this term began to be used in a more general sense. Among some philosophers it became the title of an object of worship; while, on the other hand, it degenerated into the genii of poetry and imagination.

In tracing the popular transitions and transmigrations of words, permit me, gentlemen, to say that we are not to imagine that they very ceremoniously advance, as our naval and military officers, from one rank to another, by some systematic or conventional agreement, amongst the heads of the departments in the army of words and phalanxes of human speech. On the contrary, the transitions are exceedingly anomalous, and sometimes inverted. In this instance the term *demon,* from simply indicating *a knowing one,* became the title of a human spirit when divested of the appendages of its clay tenement, because of its supposed initiation into the secrets of another world. Thus a separated spirit became a genius, a demigod, a mediator, a divinity of the ancient superstition according to its acquirements in this state of probation.

But we shall better understand the force and import of this mysterious word from its earliest acceptation among the elder Pagans, Jews, and Christians, than from the speculations of etymologists and lexicographers. Historical facts, then, and not etymological speculations, shall decide not only its meaning, but the character and rank of those beings on whom, by common consent, this significant title was conferred.

To whom, then, among Pagan writers shall we make our first appeal? Shall we not at once carry up the question to the most venerable Hesiod, the oldest of Grecian bards, whose antique style even antedates that of Homer himself almost one hundred years? Shall we not appeal to the genealogist of all the gods, the great theogonist of Grecian mythology? Who, more than he, [is] likely to be acquainted with the ancient traditions of demons? And what is the sum of his testimony in the case? Hear him speak in the words of Plutarch: "The spirits of mortals become demons when separated from their earthly bodies." The Grecian biographer not only quotes with approbation the views of Hesiod, but corroborates them with the result of his own researches, avowing his conviction that "the demons of the Greeks were the ghosts and genii of departed men; and that they go up and down the earth as observers, and even rewarders of men; and although not actors themselves, they encourage others to act in harmony with their views and characters." Zenocrates, too, as found in Aristotle, extends the term to the souls of men before death, and calls them demons while in the body. To the good demons and the spirits of deceased heroes they allotted the office of mediators between gods and men.[4] In this character Zoroaster, Thales, Pythagoras, Plato, Plutarch, Celsus, Apuleius, and many others contemplated The demons of their times.

Whoever, indeed, will be at pains to examine the Pagan mythologies, one and all, will discover that some doctrine of demons, as respects their nature, abodes, characters, or employments, is the ultimate foundation of the whole superstructure; and that the radical idea of all the dogmata of their priests, and the fancies and fables of their poets, are found in that most ancient and veritable tradition—that the spirits of men survive their fallen tabernacles, and live in a disembodied state from death to the dissolution of material nature. To these spirits in the character of genii, gods, or demigods, they assigned the fates and fortunes of men and countries. With them a hero on earth became a demon in hades; and a demigod, a numen, a divinity in the skies. It is not without some reason that the witty and ingenious Lucian makes his dialogist, in the orthodoxy of his age, thus ask and answer the following questions:—*What is man? A mortal god! And what is God? An immortal man.* In one sentence, all Pagan antiquity affirms that from Titan and Saturn, the poetic progeny of Coelus and Terra, down to Aesculapius, Proteus, and Minos, all their divinities, were the ghosts of dead men, and were so regarded by the most erudite of the Pagans themselves.

Think not, gentlemen, that because we summon the Pagan witnesses first, that we regard them either as the first in point of age or character. Far from it. They were a pack of plagiarists, from Hesiod to Lucian. The Greeks were the greatest literary thieves and robbers

---

[4] Hence the saint worship and saint mediators of the dark ages, and of the less favored portions of our Anglo Saxon race.

that ever lived, and they had the most consummate art of concealing the theft. From these Pagans, whether Greeks or Romans, we ascend to the Jews and to the Patriarchs, whose annals transcend those of the most ancient Pagans many centuries.

In the times of the Patriarchs, in the infancy of the Abrahamic family, long before the time of their own Moses, we learn that in the land of Canaan, almost coeval with the promise of it to Abraham, demons were recognized and worshipped. The consultation of the spirits of the dead, the art and mystery of necromancy, the species of familiar spirits, and wizards, are older than Moses, and spoken of by him as matters of ancient faith and veneration. Statutes, indeed, are ordained, and laws are promulged from Mount Sinai in Arabia, from the voice of the Eternal King, against the worship of demons, the consultation of familiar spirits, the practice of necromancy, and all the arts of divination; of which we may speak more particularly in the sequel. Hence we affirm that the doctrine of a separate state— of disembodied ghosts, or demons—of necromancy and divination, is a thousand years older than Homer or Hesiod, than any Pagan historian, philosopher, or poet whatsoever. And so deeply rooted in the land of Canaan, so early and so long cherished and taught by the seven nations was this doctrine in all its branches, that, notwithstanding the severe statutes against it, traces of it are found among the Jews for almost a thousand years after Moses. Of the wicked Jeroboam it is said, "He ordained priests for the high places, and for the demons.[5] Even David admits that his nation "learned the works of the heathen, served their idols, and sacrificed their sons and daughters to demons;" and he adds, "they ate the sacrifices of *the dead*," a clear intimation that worshipping demons was worshipping

---

[5] Deuteronomy 18: 10. Leviticus 17: 7, etc. 2 Chron. 11: 15. Psalm 106: 26-37.

the dead. Isaiah, too, lamenting their idolatry, asks the mortifying question, "Shall a people seek the living to the dead?"

But there is a peculiarity in the acceptation of this term among Jews and Pagans which demands special attention. Amongst them the term *demon* generally, if not universally, denoted an unclean, malign, or wicked spirit: whereas amongst the Pagans it as often represented a good as an evil spirit. Who has not heard of the good demon of Socrates, and of the evil genius of Brutus? While among Jews and Christians so commonly are found the *akatharta pneumata,* or the *ponera pneumata*—the unclean and malign spirits, that our translators have almost uniformly translated them *devils.*

In the Christian scriptures we meet the term *demon,* in one form or other, 75 times, and in such circumstances, as, with but one or two exceptions, constrain us to regard it as the representative of a wicked and unclean spirit. So general is this fact, that Beelzebub is dignified "*The Prince of the Demons*"—unfortunately rendered *devils.* This frequency of immoral and wicked associations with the word *daimoon* may have induced our translators to give us so many *devils* in their authorized version. But this misapprehension is now universally admitted and regretted: for while the Bible teaches many demons, it nowhere intimates a plurality of Devils or Satans. There is but one Devil or Satan in the universe, whose legions 'of angels and demons give him a sort of omnipresence, by acting out his will in all their intercourse with mortals. This evil spirit, whose official titles are the Serpent, the Devil, and Satan, is always found in the singular number in both the Hebrew and Greek scriptures; while *demon* is found in both numbers, indicating sometimes one, and sometimes a legion.

But that we may not be farther tedious in this dry work of definition, and that we may enter at once upon the subject with a zeal and spirit worthy of a topic which lays the axe at the root of the tree of modern Sadduceesism, Materialism, and Skepticism, we shall proceed at once to sum up the evidence in proof of the proposition which we shall state as the peculiar theme of this great literary adventure.—That proposition is—*The demons of Paganism, Judaism, and Christianity were the ghosts of dead men.*

But some of you may say, You have proposed to dismiss this work of definition too soon: for here is the horrible word *ghost!* Of what is that term the sign in your style? Well, we must explain ourselves.

Our Saxon forefathers, of whom we have no good reason to be ashamed, were wont to call the spirits of men, especially when separated from their bodies, *ghosts.* This, however, they did, not with the terrible associations which arise in our minds on every pronunciation of that startling term. *Guest* and *ghost,* with them, if not synonyms, were, at least, cousins-german. They regarded the body as the *house,* and therefore called the spirit the *guest;* for guest and ghost are two branches from the same root. William Tyndale, the martyr, of excellent memory, in his version of the New Testament, the prototype of that of king James, very judiciously makes the Holy Spirit of the Old Testament the Holy Ghost of the New; because, in his judgment, it was the promised guest of the Christian temple.

Still it is difficult, I own, to hear the word ghost, or demon, without the recollection of the nursery tales and fictions of our irrational systems of early education. We suffer little children to hear so much of

> "Apparitions tall and ghastly,
> That take their stand o'er some new-opened grave,
> And, strange to tell, evanish at the crowing of the
> cock,"

till they become not only in youth, but often in riper years, the prey and sport of idle fears and terrors "which scarce the firm philosopher can scorn." Not only the graveyard,

"But the lonely tower
Is also shunn'd, whose mournful chronicles hold,
So night-struck fancy dreams, the yelling ghost!"

Imagination once startled,

"In grim array the nightly specters rise!
Oft have we seen the school-boy, with satchel in his hand,
When passing by some haunted spot, at lonely ev'n,
Whistling aloud to bear his courage up. Suddenly he hears,
Or thinks he hears, the sound of something purring at his heels:

Full fast he flies, nor does tie took behind him,
Till out of breath he o'ertake his fellows,
Who gather round and wonder at the tale!"

Parents are greatly at fault for permitting such tales to disturb the fancies of their infant offspring. The love of the marvelous and of the supernatural is so deeply planted in human nature, that it needs but little cultivation to make it fruitful in all manner of fairy tales, of ghosts and specters. But there is an opposite extreme—the denial of spirits, angels, demons, whether good or bad. Here, too, *media ibis tutissima*—the middle path the safer is. But to our proposition: We have, from a careful survey of the history of the term *demon*, concluded that *the demons of Paganism, Judaism, and Christianity were the ghosts of dead men.* But we build not only upon the definition of the term, nor on its philological history; but upon the following seven pillars:

1. All the Pagan authors of note, whose works have survived the wreck of ages, affirm the opinion that demons were the spirits or ghosts of dead men. From Hesiod down to the more polished

Celsus, their historians, poets, and philosophers occasionally express this opinion.

2. The Jewish historians, Josephus and Philo, also avow this conviction. Josephus says, "Demons are the spirits of wicked men, who enter into living men and destroy them, unless they are so happy as to meet with speedy relief.[6] Philo says, "The souls of dead men are called demons."

3. The Christian Fathers, Justin Martyr, Irenaeus, Origen, etc. depose to the same effect. Justin, when arguing for a future state, alleges, "Those who are seized and tormented by the souls of the dead, whom all call demons, and madmen."[7] Lardner, after examining with the most laborious care the works of these, and all the Fathers of the first two centuries, says, "The notion of demons, or the souls of dead men, having power over living men, was *universally* prevalent among the heathen of these times, and believed by many Christians.[8]

4. The Evangelists and Apostles of Jesus Christ so understood the matter. As this is a very important, and of itself a sufficient pillar on which to rest our edifice, we shall be at more pains to illustrate and enforce it. We shall first state the philological law or canon of criticism, on the generality and truth of which all our dictionaries, grammars, and translations are formed. *Every word*

---

[6] De Bello Jud. cap. 8: 25; cap. 6: sect 3.

[7] Jus. Apology, b. 1: p. 65, par. 12, p. 54.

[8] Vol. 8: P. 368.

not specially explained or defined in a particular sense, by any standard writer of any particular age and country, is to be taken and applied in the current or commonly received signification of that country and age in which the writer lived and wrote. If this canon of translation and of criticism be denied, then we affirm there is no value in dictionaries, nor in the acquisition of ancient languages in which any book may be written; nor is there any confidence in any translation of any ancient work, sacred or profane: for they are all made upon the assumption of the truth of this law.

We have then only to ask first for the current signification of this term *demon* in Judea at the Christian era; and, in the second place, Did the inspired writers ever give any special definition of it? We have already found an answer to the first in the Greeks and Jews of the apostolic age—also, in the preceding and subsequent age. We have heard Josephus, Philo, Lucian, Justin, and Lardner, from whose writings and affirmations we are expressly told what the universal acceptation of the term was in Judea and in those times; and in the second place, the Apostles and our Lord, as already said, use this word in various forms 75 times, and on no occasion give any hint of a special, private, or peculiar interpretation of it; which was not their method when they used a term either not generally understood, or understood in a special sense. Does anyone ask the meaning of the word Messiah, prophet, priest, elder, deacon, presbytery, altar, sacrifice, Sabbath, circumcision, etc. etc.? We refer him to the current signification of these words among the Jews and Greeks of that age. Why, then, should anyone except the term *demon* from the universal law? Are we not, therefore, sustained by the highest and most authoritative decision of that literary tribunal by whose rules and decrees all works sacred and profane are translated from a dead to a living tongue? We are, then, fully authorized to say that the demons of the New Testament were the spirits of dead men.

5. But as a distinct evidence of the historic kind, and rather as confirmatory of our views than of the authority of the inspired authors, I adduce as a separate and independent witness a very explicit and decisive passage from the epistle to the Smyrneans, written by the celebrated Ignatius, the disciple of the Apostle John. He quotes the words of the Lord to Peter when Peter supposed he saw a spirit or a ghost. But he quotes him thus—"Handle me and see, for I am not a *daimoon asomaton*—a disembodied demon;"—a spirit without a body. This places the matter above all doubt that with them of that day a demon and a ghost were equivalent terms.

6. But we also deduce an argument from the word *angel*. This word is of Bible origin, and confined to those countries in which that volume is found. It is not found in all the Greek poets, orators, or historians, so far as known to me. Of that rank of beings to whom Jews and Christians have applied this official title, the Pagan nations seem never to have had the first conception. It is therefore certain that they could not use the term *demon* as a substitute interchangeable with the word *angel*—as indicative of an intermediate order of intelligent beings above men, and between them and the Divinity. They had neither the name nor the idea of an angel in their mythology. Philo the Jew has, indeed, said that amongst the Jews the word *demon* and the word *angel* were sometimes used interchangeably; and some have thence inferred lapsed angels were called demons. But this is not a logical inference: for the Jews called the winds, the pestilence, the lightnings of heaven, etc., *angels,* as indicative of their agency in accomplishing the will of God. In this sense, indeed, a demon

might be officially called an angel. But in this sense demon is to angel as the species to the genus: we can call a demon an angel, but we cannot call an angel a demon—just as we can call every man an animal, but we cannot call every animal a man.

Others, indeed, have just as fancifully imagined that the old *giants* and *heroes,* said to have been the fruit of the intermarriage of the sons of God with the daughters of men before the flood, were the demons of all the world—Pagans, Jews, and Christians. Their most plausible argument is, that the word *heroes* and the word *love* are the same; and that the *loves* of the angels for the daughters of men, was the reason that their gigantic offspring were called *heroes.* Whence the term was afterwards appropriated to persons of great courage as well as of great stature. This is sublimely ridiculous.

But to return to the word *angel.* It is a Bible term, and not being found in all classic, in all mythological antiquity, could not enter into the Pagan ideas of a demon. Now that it is not so used in the Christian scriptures is evident for the following reasons:

1st Angels were never said to enter into any one.

2nd Angels have, no affection for bodies of any sort, either as habitations or vehicles of action.

3rd Angels have no predilection for tombs and monuments of the dead.

In these three particulars angels and demons stand in full contrast, and are contradistinguished by essentially different characteristics: for—

1st. Demons have entered into human bodies and into the bodies of inferior creatures.

2d. Demons evince a peculiar affection for human bodies, and seem to desire them both as vehicles of action and as places of habitation.

3d. Demons also evince a peculiar fondness for their old mortal tenements: hence we so often read of them carrying the possessed into the grave-yards, the tombs, and sepulchers, where, perchance, their old mortalities lay in ruins.

From which facts we argue, as well as from the fact that the Pagans had neither Devil, nor angel nor Satan, in their heads before the Christian times, that when they, or the Christians, or the Jews spoke of *demons,* they could not mean any intermediate rank of spirits, other than the spirits of dead men. Hence in no instance in holy writ can we find *demon* and *angel* used as convertible terms. Is it not certain, then, that they are the ghosts of dead men?—But there yet remains another pillar.

7. Among the evidences of the papal defection intimated by Paul, he associates the *doctrine concerning demons* with celibacy and abstinence from certain meats, as chief among the signs of that fearful apostasy. He warrants the conclusion that the purgatorial prisons for ghosts and the ghostly mediators of departed saints, which, equally with commanding to abstain from lawful meats, and forbidding to marry, characterize the times of which he spoke, are attributes of the same system, and indicative of the fact that *demons* and *ghosts* are two names for the same beings. To this we add the testimony of James, who says *the demons believe and tremble* for their doom. Now all eminent critics concur that the spirits of wicked men are here intended; and need I

add that oft-repeated affirmation of the demoniacs, "We know thee, Jesus of Nazareth; art thou come to torment us before the time?" Thus all the scriptural allusions to this subject authorize the conclusion that demons are ghosts, and especially wicked and unclean spirits of dead men. A single saying in the Apocalypse makes this most obvious. When Babylon is razed to its foundation it is said to be made the habitation of demons—of the ghosts of its sepulchered inhabitants. From these seven sources of evidence, viz.—the Pagan authors, the Jewish historians, the Christian fathers, the four Evangelists, the epistle of Ignatius, the acceptation of the term *angel* in its contrast with *demon,* and the internal evidences of the whole New Testament, we conclude that the demons of the New Testament were the ghosts of wicked men. May we not henceforth reason from this point with all assurance as a fixed and fundamental principle?

It ought, however, to be candidly stated that there have been in latter times a few intellectual dyspeptics, on whose nervous system the idea of being really possessed by an evil spirit, produces a frenzied excitement. Terrified at the thought of an incarnate demon, they have resolutely undertaken to prove that every single demon named in holy writ is but a bold eastern metaphor, placing in high relief dumbness, deafness, madness, palsy, epilepsy, etc.; and hence demoniacs then and now are a class of unfortunates laboring under certain physical maladies called unclean spirits. *Credat Judæus Appella, non Ego.*

On the principle that every demon is an eastern metaphor, how incomparably more eloquent than Demosthenes or Cicero, was he that had at one time a legion of eastern metaphors within him struggling for utterance! No wonder, then, that the swineherds of Gadara were overwhelmed by the moving eloquence of their herds as they rushed with such pathos into the deep waters of the dark Galilee!

Great men are not always wise. The seer of 'Mesopotamia was not only admonished, but reformed by the eloquence of an ass; and I am sure that the Gadarene speculators were cured of their belief in eastern metaphors when they saw their hopes of gain forever buried in the lake of Gennesereth. It requires a degree of gravity bordering on the superlative, to speculate on an hypothesis so singularly fanciful and baseless as that which converts both reason and eloquence, deafness and dumbness, into one and the same metaphor.

Without impairing in the least the strength of the arguments in favor of actual possession by the spirits of dead men, it may be conceded, that because of the similarity of some of the effects of demoniacal possession with those maladies of the paralytic and epileptic character, it may have happened on some occasions that persons simply afflicted with these diseases, because of the difficulties of always discriminating the remote causes of these maladies, were, by the common people, regarded as demoniacs, and so reported in the New Testament. Still the fact that the Great Teacher himself distinguishes between demons and all human maladies, in commanding the Apostles not only to "heal all manner of diseases—to cleanse the lepers, and raise the dead;" but also to "cast out demons;" and the fact still more palpable, that in number and power these demons are represented as transcending all physical maladies, precludes the possibility of contemplating them as corporeal diseases.

"When I read of the number of demons in particular persons," says a very distinguished Biblical critic," and see their actions expressly distinguished from those of the man possessed; conversations held by the demons about their disposal after their expulsion; and accounts given how they were actually disposed of; when I find desires and passions ascribed peculiarly to them; and similitudes taken from their manners and customs, it is impossible for me to deny their existence, without admitting that the sacred historians were themselves deceived in regard to them, or intended to deceive their readers."

Were it not in appearance like killing those that are dead, I should quote at length sundry passages which speak of "unclean spirits *crying with loud voices*" as they came out of many that were possessed, which represent unclean spirits falling down before Jesus, and crying, "Thou art the Son of God," and of Jesus "charging them not to make him known;" but I will only cite a single parable framed upon the case of a demoniac. It is reported by Matthew and Luke, and almost in the same words. "When the unclean spirit," says Jesus, "is gone out of a man, he walks through dry places, seeking rest and finding none. Then he says, I will return into my house from whence I came out; and when he is come he finds it empty, swept, and garnished. Then he goes and takes with himself seven other spirits more wicked than himself, and they enter in and dwell there; and the last state of that man is worse than the first. Even so shall it be also to this wicked generation." On which observe, that "unclean spirits" is another name for demons—that is, a metaphor of a metaphor; for if demons are metaphors for diseases, the unclean spirits are metaphors of metaphors, or shadows of shades. Again, the Great Teacher is found not only for once departing from himself, but also from all human teachers of renown, in basing a parable upon a parable, or a shadow upon a shade, in drawing a similitude from a simile. His object was to illustrate the last state of the Jews. This he attempts by the adventures of a demon—first being dispossessed, finding no rest, and returning with others more wicked than himself to the man from whom he was driven. Now if this was all a figure to illustrate a figure, the Savior has done that which he never before attempted, inasmuch as his parables are all founded not upon fictions, but upon facts—upon the actual manners and customs, the incidents and usages of society.

That must be a desperate position to sustain which degrades the Savior as a teacher below the rank of the most ordinary instructors of any age. The last state of the Jews compared to a metaphor!—compared to a nonentity!—compared to a fiction! This is even worse than representing a trope coming out of a man's mouth, "crying with a loud voice," "wandering through dry places"—unfigurative language, I presume— seeking a period, and finding a comma. At length, tired and fatigued, returning with seven fiercer metaphors more wickedly eloquent than himself, re-possessing the orator, and making him internally more eloquent than before. It will not help the matter to say that when a disease leaves a man it wanders through dry or wet places—through marshes and fens—through deserts and prairies—and finding no rest for its foot, takes with him seven other more violent diseases, and seeks for the unfortunate man from whom the Doctors expelled it; and, re-entering his improved constitution, makes that its eternal abode.

In one sentence, then, we conclude that there is neither reason nor fact—there is no canon of criticism, no law of interpretation—there is nothing in human experience or observation—there is nothing in all antiquity, sacred or profane, that, in our judgment, weighs against the evidence already adduced in support of the position, that *the demons of Pagans, Jews, and Christians were the ghosts of dead men; and, as such, have taken possession of men's living bodies, and have moved, influenced, and impelled them to certain courses of action.*

Permit me, gentlemen, to demonstrate that this is no abstract and idle speculation, by stating a few of the practical aspects and bearings of this doctrine of demonology:

1st It relieves the Bible from the imputation of promulging laws against non-entities in all its legislation against necromancers, diviners, soothsayers, wizards, fortune-tellers, etc. When Jehovah gave this law to Israel, he legislated not against mere pretenses, saying, "You shall not permit to live among, you any one that uses divination, an enchanter, a witch, a consulter of familiar spirits, a wizard, or a necromancer; for all that do these things are an abomination to the Lord: and because of these abominations the Lord thy God doth drive these nations out before thee." A divine law demanding capital punishment because of a mere pretense! The most incredible thing in the world! The existence of such a statute, as before intimated, implies not merely the antiquity of the fact of demoniacal influence, but supposes it so palpable that it could be proved by at least two witnesses, and so satisfactorily as to authorize the taking away of human life without the risk of shedding innocent blood.

That there have been pretenders to such mysterious arts, impostors and hypocrites in necromancy, witchcraft, and divination, as well as in everything else, I doubt not; but if the pretense to work a miracle, or to utter a prediction, be a proof that there were true miracles and true prophets, the pretense of necromancy, witchcraft, and divination, is also a proof that there were once true necromancers, wizards, and diviners. The fame of the Egyptian Jannes and Jambres who withstood Moses in the presence of Pharaoh—the fame of the woman of Endor, who evoked Samuel, or someone that personated him—and of the Pythonic damsel that followed Paul and Barnabas, and who enriched her master by her divination, stand on the pages of eternal truth imperishable monuments not merely of the antiquity of the pretense, but of the reality of demoniacal power and possession.

May I be permitted farther to observe on this mysterious subject, that necromancy was the principal parent of all the arts of divination ever practiced in the world, and was directly and avowedly founded on the fact, not only of demoniacal influence, but that demons are the spirits of dead men, with whom living men could, and did form intimacies. This the very word *necromancy* intimates. The necromancer predicted the future by means of demoniacal inspiration. He was a prophet inspired by the dead. His art lay in making or finding a familiar spirit, in evoking a demon from whom he obtained superhuman knowledge. So the Greek term imports and all antiquity confirms.

There are two subjects on which God is silent, and man most solicitous to know—the world of spirits, and his own future destiny. On these two subjects ghosts who have visited the unseen world, and whose horizon is so much enlarged, are supposed to be peculiarly intelligent, and on this account originally called *demons,* or *knowing ones.* But this knowledge being forbidden, kindly forbidden man, to seek it at all, and especially by unlawful means, has always been obnoxious to the anathema of Heaven. Hence the popularity of the profession of evoking familiar spirits, and hence also the indignation of Heaven against them who consulted them.

Still we will be asked, Has any spirit of man, dead or alive, power to foresee and foretell the future? Does anyone know the future but God? To which we cheerfully respond, The living and inspired prophets only knew a part of the future. God alone knows all the future. But angels or demons may know much more of it than man. How this may be analogy itself may suggest Suppose, for example, that one man possessed the discriminating powers of a Bacon, a Newton, or a Locke, only of a more capacious and retentive memory, had been coeval with Cain, Noah, or Abraham, and with a deathless vigor of constitution had lived with all the generations of men since their day till now, an inductive philosopher of course; what would be his comparative power of calculating chances and contingencies—the laws of cause and effect—and of thence anticipating the future? Still, compared with one who had passed that mysterious borne of time, he would be but the infant of a day, knowing comparatively nothing of human destiny. But, indeed, the powers of knowing peculiar to disembodied spirits, are to us as inscrutable as the very elements of their spiritual forms and existence. But that they do know more of a spiritual system and more of human destiny than we, all antiquity sacred and profane fully reveals and confirms.

2nd But a second practical aspect of this theory of demons demands our attention. ***It is a palpable and irrefragable proof of a spiritual system.***

The gross materialists of the French school, when Atheism triumphed over reason and faith, proclaimed from their own metropolis, and had it cut deep in marble too, that death was an eternal sleep of body, soul, and spirit, in one common unconsciousness of being. Since that time we have had the subject somewhat refined and sublimated into an intermediate sleep of only some six or seven thousand years, between our earthly exit and the resurrection morn. These more speculative materialists convert demons into metaphors, lapsed angels, or devils—into anything rather than the living spirits of dead men.

They see that our premises being admitted, there must be a renunciation not only of the grosser, but of the more ethereal forms of materialism of those who lull the spirit to repose in the same sepulcher with its kindred mortality, in their opposition to the inhabitation of the human body by any other spirit than its own. They make but little argumentative gain who assume that demons are lapsed angels rather than human ghosts: for who will not admit that it may be more easy for a demon than an angel who has a spiritual body of his own, to work by the machinery of a human body, and to excite the human passions to any favorite course of action! Were not this the fact, they must have tenanted the human house to little purpose, if a perfect stranger to all its rooms and doors could, on its first introduction, move through them as readily as they.

"If weak thy faith, why choose the harder side?"

To allegorize demoniacal influences, or to metamorphose them into rhetorical imagery, is the shortest, though the most desperate escape, from all spiritual embarrassment in the case. But the harder you press the skeptical philosopher on the subject of his peculiar idolatry, the more bold his denial of all spiritual influences, celestial or infernal; and the more violently he affirms that demoniacal possessions were physical diseases; that necromancy, familiar spirits, and divination, though older than Moses, and the seven nations of Canaan, were but mere pretenses; an imposition on the credulity of man, as idle as the legends of Salem witchcraft, or the fairy tales of the mother-land of sprites and apparitions. But this, let me tell you, skeptical philosopher, relieves not the hard destiny of your case. Whether necromancy in all its forms was real or pretended, true or false, affects not the real merits of the question before us.

To me, in this branch of the argument, it is perfectly indifferent whether it was a pretense or a reality: for, mark it well, had there not been a senior and more venerated belief in the existence of a spiritual system—a general persuasion that the spirits of the dead lived in another world while their bodies lay in this, and that disembodied spirits were demons or knowing ones on those peculiar points so interesting and so unapproachable to man; who ever could have thought of consulting them, of evoking them by any art, or of pretending in the face of the world to any familiarity with them! I gain strength by the denial or by the admission of the thing, so long as its high antiquity must be conceded. I do indeed contend, and will contend, that a belief in demons, in a separate existence of the spirits of the dead, is more ancient than necromancy, and that it is a belief and a tradition older than the Pagan, the Jewish, or the Christian systems—older than Moses and his law—older than any earthly record whatever.

Not a few of our modern sages ascribe to a Pagan origin that which antedates Paganism itself. They must have a Grecian, Roman, or Egyptian origin for ideas, usages, and institutions existent ages before the founders of these states or the inventors of their superstitions were born. No earthly record, the Bible alone excepted, reaches within hundreds of years of the origin of the idea of demons, necromancy, and of infernal as well as of supernal agency.

Others there are who have more faith in what is modern than in what is ancient. They would rather believe their children than their fathers. The moderns, indeed, in most of the physical sciences, and in some of the physical arts, greatly excel the ancients. I say, in some of the useful and fine arts we may, perhaps, excel them as much as they excelled us in geometry, architecture, sculpture, painting, poetry, etc. etc. But though we excel them so much in many new discoveries and arts—in correct, traditional, and spiritual knowledge they greatly excelled us; except always that portion of the moderns fully initiated into the mysteries of the Bible. Some seem to reason as if they thought that the farther from the fountain the waters are more pure—the longer the channel the freer from pollution. With me the reverse is the fact. Man was more intelligent at his creation and his fall in his own being and destiny than he has ever been since, except so far as he has been the subject of a new revelation. Would it not appear waste of time to attempt to prove that our national government is purer now than it was while its founders were all living amongst us? Equally prodigal of time the man who attempts to prove that the Patriarchal, Jewish and Christian institutions were purer five hundred or a thousand years after, than at, their commencement. With Tertullian I will say, that in faith, religion, and morality, whatever is most ancient is most true. Therefore the Patriarchs knew more of man living and dead, of the ancient order of things in nature, society, and art, than we their remote posterity.

The age of philosophy was the era of hypotheses and doubts. Man never began to form hypothesis till he lost his way. Now having traced the belief in demons and necromancy beyond the age of conjecture and speculative reasoning, and located it amongst the oldest traditions in the world, we are compelled by the dicta of our own inductive and sounder philosophy to admit its claims to an experience, observation, and testimony properly authenticated and documented amongst the earliest fathers of mankind. One of the oracles of true science is, that *all, our ideas are the result of sensation and reflection, or of experience and observation;* that the archetypes of all our natural impressions and views are found in material nature; and therefore man could as easily create a world as a ghost, either by imagination, volition, or reason. Supernatural ideas must therefore have a supernatural origin. So speaks the Baconian system, and therefore its author believed in demons, spirits, and necromancy, as much as your humble servant, or any other living Baconian.

When any man proves he can have faith without hearing and testimony—the idea of color without sight—or of hardness and softness, of heat and cold, without feeling, and understand all the properties of material nature, without any of his five senses, then, *but not till then,* he may explain how, without a supernatural influence of any sort, he may form either the idea or the name of a spirit, a ghost, or a demon—of a spiritual, invisible, and eternal system of intelligences of a supernatural mold and temper. He that can create out of himself the idea of an abstract spirit, or of a spiritual system of any sort, may create matter by volition, and a universe out of nothing.

Dispose of the matter as she may, we affirm it as our conviction that Philosophy herself is compelled to admit the existence of demons, familiar spirits, and the arts of necromancy and divination, which all ancient literature and ancient tradition—all Patriarchal, Jewish, and Christian records assert. In this instance, as in many others, faith is easier than unbelief; and Reason voluntarily places herself by the side of Faith as her handmaid and coadjutor in sustaining a spiritual system, of which demons in their proper nature and character are an irrefragable proof.

3rd A third practical tendency of this view of demoniacal influence is ***to exalt in our esteem the character of the Supreme Philanthropist***.

We will be asked, Whence have all the demons fled? What region do they now inhabit! Have they not power to possess mankind as formerly? Is necromancy, divination, and witchcraft forever exiled from the abodes of men?

Many such questions there may be propounded, which neither philosophy, nor experience, nor religion do infallibly determine. But we may say in general and in truthful terms, that the heralds of salvation, from the day of their first mission to the end of their evangelical labors, were casting out demons, restraining Satanic influence, and making inroads upon the power and empire of Beelzebub, the Prince of the Demons. The mighty chieftain of this holy war had a personal encounter with the malignant chief of all unclean spirits, angelic and human, and so defeated his counsels and repelled his assaults as to divest him of much of his sway, as a presage and earnest of his ultimate triumph over all the powers of darkness. His success and that of his ambassadors on two occasions called from his lips two oracles of much consolation to all his friends; "I saw," said he, "Satan fall like lightning from heaven." This he spake when they told him, "The demons are subject to us through thy word." "Behold," he adds, "I give you power to tread on serpents and scorpions, and on all the power of the enemy, and nothing shall by any means hurt you." The partial dethronement of Satan, Prince of the Demons, is here fully indicated. The Roman orator uses this style when speaking of Pompey's overthrow. His words are, "He has fallen from the stars." And again, of the fall of the colleague of Antonius—"Thou hast pulled him down from heaven." So spake the Messiah: "I beheld Satan as lightning fall from heaven." His empire over men from that day began to fall. And on another occasion he says, "Now is the Prince of this world cast out." These, together with other similar indications, allow the conclusion that the power of demons is wholly destroyed as far as Christians are concerned; and if not wholly, greatly restrained in all lands where the gospel has found its way. With an old prophet or diviner who tried his hand against God's people once, we may say, "There is no enchantment against Jacob—there is no divination against Israel." Some arrogate to human science what has been the prerogative of the gospel alone. They say the light of science has driven ghosts and witches from the minds of men; whereas they ought to have said, the gospel and power of its Author have driven demons out of the hearts, and dispossessed them of their power over the bodies of men.

The error of these admirers of human science is not much different from that of some European theologians concerning Mary Magdalene. They suppose her to have been an infamous, rather than an unfortunate woman, out of whom were driven seven devils. They have disgraced her memory by erecting 'Magdalene Hospitals' for infamous, rather than for unfortunate females; not knowing that it was the misfortune, rather than the crime of Mary of Magdala, that seven demons had been permitted to assault her person for the glory of the Messiah and her own eternal fame.

As to the abodes of the demons, we are taught in the Bible what the most ancient dogmatists have said concerning their residence in the air: I say we are taught that they dwell *pro tempore* in the ethereal regions. Satan, their Prince, is called "the Prince of the power of the air." The great Apostle to the Gentiles taught them to wrestle against "wicked spirits that reside in the air;" for, says he, "you fight not against flesh and blood, but against principalities and powers, against the rulers of the darkness of this world; against spiritual wickedness in high places"—properly rendered, '*Against wicked spirits in the regions of the air.*' Paul's shipwreck at Malta by the Euroclydon, and Job's misfortunes by an Arabian tempest, demonstrate the aerial power of this great antagonist when permitted to exert it against those he envies and calumniates.

Evident it is, then, from such testimonies, facts, and allusions, that the atmosphere, or rather the regions above it, the ethereal or empyreal, and not heaven, nor earth, nor hell, is the proper residence of the ghosts of wicked men. They have repeatedly declared their perfect punishment or torment as yet future, and after the coming of the Lord, when he shall send the Devil and his emissaries into an eternal fire. How often did they say to Jesus, "Art thou come to torment us *before the time?*" That they are miserable, wretchedly miserable, is inferable from the abhorrence of the nudity and awful forebodings of their present position. They vehemently desire to be embodied again. They seek rest, but find none; and would rather possess any bodies, even the swine, than continue naked and dispossessed. Their prison is called by the Messiah, "outer darkness;" by Paul it is called *epourania, high places, aerial regions.* This is the, Hebrew-Greek name of that region where there is neither atmosphere nor light; for, strange though it may appear to uneducated minds, the limits of our atmosphere are the limits of all terrestrial light. These intervals between the atmospheres of the planets is what we would call "*outer darkness.*" Could a person ascend only some fifty miles above this earth, he would find himself surrounded with everlasting night—no ray from sun, or moon, or stars could find him where there is no medium of reflection.

That they may still inspire oracles, as they were wont before the Christian era—(this, too, has been counterfeited)—and possess living men in heathen lands, or in places where Christianity has made little progress, is not altogether improbable. Of this, indeed, we have not satisfactory evidence, and therefore ought not to speak dogmatically. I know many affect to regard the whole matter as a piece of childish superstition, as did our two last great poets, Scott and Byron; who, nevertheless, like them, are under the influence of that same childish superstition. One thing is abundantly evident and satisfactory—that although the number of such spirits is vast and overwhelming, and although their hatred to the living is intense and enduring, the man of God, the true Christian, has a guardian angel, or a host of sentinels around him that never sleep; and, therefore, against him the fiery darts of Satan and the wiles of the roaring lion are employed in vain. For this we erect in our hearts a monument of thanks to Him who has been, and still is, the Supreme Philanthropist and Redeemer of our race.

This view of demonology not only vindicates the law of Moses from the imputation of catering to the superstitious prejudices of mankind, by regarding as real the most idle fictions and pretenses; and justifies Paul in placing witchcraft amongst the works of the flesh; it not only affords to weak and doubting minds new and striking evidences of a spiritual system; it not only develops our great indebtedness to the Author of the Christian faith in rescuing man from the tyranny of the arch apostate, the Prince of Demons; but it also inducts us into still more grand and sublime views of the magnitude, variety, and extent of the world of spirits—of our relations to them—and throws some light upon our present liabilities to impressions, suggestions, and influences from classes of agents wholly invisible and inappreciable by any of those senses which connect us with external and sensible existence.

That we are susceptible of impressions and suggestions from invisible agents sometimes affecting our passions and actions, it were foolish and infidel to deny. How many thousands of well authenticated facts are found in the volumes of human experience of singular, anomalous, and inexplicable impulses and impressions wholly beyond all human associations of ideas, yet leading to actions evidently essential to the salvation of the subjects of them, or of others under their care, from imminent perils and disasters; to which, but for such kind offices, they must inevitably have fallen victims. And how many in the midst of a wicked and foolish career have, by some malign agency, been suddenly and unexpectedly led into the most fatal coincidences and suddenly precipitated to ruin, when such unprecedented exigencies are exceptions to all the known laws of cause and effect, and inexplicable to all their wonted courses of action! To assign to these any other than a spiritual cause, it seems to me, were to assign a *non causa pro causa;* for on no theory of mind or body can they be so satisfactorily explained, and so much in harmony with the Bible way of representing such incidents. Thus the angel of the Lord smote Herod that he died, and in various dreams admonished the faithful of the ways and means of escaping impending evils.

Will it not be perceived and admitted that if evil demons can enter into men's bodies, and even take away reason, as well as excite to various preternatural actions, and if in legions they may crowd their influences upon one unhappy victim, spirits, either good or bad, may make milder and more delicate approaches to the fountains of human action, and stir men up to efforts and enterprises for weal or woe, according to their respective characters and ruling passions.

Certain it is that angels, beings, too, of a more embodied and less abstract existence, have not only demonstrated their ability to assume the human form, but to exert such influence upon the outward man as to prompt him to immediate action—as in the case of Peter, who was suddenly stricken on the side by the hand of an angel when fast asleep between a Roman guard, and roused to action. The gates and bars of the prison open at his approach and shut on his escape, touched by the same hand; and thus the Apostle is rescued from the malice of his foes.

What an extended view of the intellectual and moral universe opens to our contemplation from this point! We see an outward, visible, and immense expanse everywhere, studded with constellations of suns and their attendant systems, circling in unmeasured orbits around one invisible and omnipotent center that controls them all. Amazed and overwhelmed at these stupendous displays of creative power, wisdom, and goodness, in adoring ecstasy we inquire into the uses of these mighty orbs, which, in such untold millions, diversify and adorn those undefined fields of ethereal beauty that limit our ideas of an unbounded and inconceivable space.

Reasoning from all our native analogies, and from the scattering rays of supernal light that have from suns unseen reached our world, we must infer that all these orbs are the mansions of social beings, of every conceivable variety of intelligence, capacity, and employment; and that in organized hierarchies, thrones, principalities, and lordships, they constitute each within itself an independent world; of which societies we are allowed to conclude that there are as many varieties of intellectual and moral organization and development as there are planets for their residence.

In all these intellectual assemblages, spread over the area of universal being, there are but two distinct and essentially diverse confederations—one under the rightful sovereignty of Messiah the Lord of all, and the other under the usurped dominion of that antagonist spirit of insubordination and self-will which has spread over our planet all the anarchy and misrule, all the darkness and gloom, all the sorrow and death which have embittered life, and made countless millions groan in spirit and sigh for a discharge from a conflict between good and evil, pleasure and pain, so unequal and oppressive.

This rebel angel, of such singular and mysterious character, is always found in the singular number—as *the Satan, the Devil,* and *the Apollyon* of our race. With him are confederate all disloyal spirits that have conspired against Heaven's own will in adoration of their own. In reference to this usurper and his angelic allies against the Lord's Anointed, we are obliged to consider those unhappy spirits, who, during their incarnation, took sides with him in his mad rebellion against the Eternal King. The number of angels that took part with him in his original conspiracy remains amongst the secrets of eternity, and is not to be divulged till the Devil and his angels, for whom Tophet was of old prepared, shall be separated from the social systems of the universe, and publicly sentenced to the bottomless gulf of irremediable ruin.

The whole human race, at one time or other, have been involved in this war against Heaven. Many have, indeed, deserted the dark banners of Beelzebub, and have become sons of light. Hitherto, alas! the great majority have perished in the field of rebellion, and gone down to the pit with all their armor on. These spirits, shown to be the demons of all antiquity, sacred and profane, are now a component part of the empire of Satan, and as much under his control as the original conspirators that took part with him in his primeval defection and rebellion.

How numerous they are, and how concentrated in their efforts, may be gleaned from sundry allusions in the inspired writings, especially from the melancholy history of the unfortunate Gadarene who dwelt among the tombs, tortured by a legion of them—not, perhaps, by six thousand demons in full tale, according to the full standard of a Roman legion; but by an indefinite and immense multitude. How innumerable, then, the agents demoniacal and angelic on Satan's side! What hosts of fallen men and fallen angels have conspired against the happiness of God's moral empire! No wonder that Satan is sometimes spoken of as omnipresent! If Napoleon in the day of his power, while in the palace of the Thuilleries, was said to be at work in Spain, in Portugal, in Belgium, and in France at the same time—with how much less of the figurative, and more of the literal, may Satan, whose agents are incomparably more multitudinous and diversified, as well as of vastly superior agility and power, be represented as wielding a sort of omnipresent power in all parts of our terraqueous habitation? And how malignant too!! The fabled Furies themselves were not more fierce than those unclean and mischievous spirits whose sweetest pleasure it was to torture with the most convulsive agonies those unhappy victims whom they chose to mark out for themselves.

But here we must pause: and with this awful group of exasperated and malicious demons in our horizon, it is some relief to remember that there are many good spirits of our race, allied with ten thousand times ten thousand, and thousands of thousands of angels of light, all of whom are angels of mercy and sentinels of defense around the dwellings of the righteous, the true *elite* of our race. These we learn, from high authority, are ministering spirits waiting on the heirs of salvation. These attending spirits know our spiritual foes, and are able to cope with them: for when Satan and Michael fought for the body of Moses the fallen seraph was driven to the wall and lost the day. For how many services rendered, for how many deliverances from evil spirits and from physical disasters, we are indebted to the good and benevolent, though invisible agents around us, will never be known, and therefore never told on earth; but it may nevertheless be known and told hereafter.

And with what unspeakable pleasure may some happy being in this assembly yet sit down, side by side, with his own guardian spirit under the eternally verdant boughs of the life-restoring tree in the paradise of God, and listen to the ten thousand deliverances effected for him by the kind ministrations of that generous and beneficent minister of grace, that watched his path, numbered his steps, and encamped around his bed from the first to the last moment of his terrestrial day! With what grateful emotions will the ransomed spirit listen to the bold adventures and the triumphant encounters with belligerent foes, of his kind and successful deliverer; and while, in the midst of such social raptures he throws his immortal arms around his kind benefactor, he lifts his bright and beaming eye of grateful piety to Him who gave him such a friend and deliverer in the time of peril and of need; and who, through such a scene of trials and of conflicts, brought him safely to the peaceful city of eternal rest!

Note

The preceding essay bears the impress or an almost extemporaneous effusion on a subject requiring much and profound thought. The invitation to address *The Popular Lecture Club* of the city of Nashville, was received but a few evenings before its pronunciation. Meanwhile, having almost daily lectures on portions of the Christian system, I had leisure only to sketch, with much rapidity, at various intervals, the preceding remarks. True, indeed, the subject had been often on my mind, especially since the time of my writing a few essays on that skeptical and abstract something called *Materialism.* The facts and observations crowded together in this popular lecture are matters of grave and serious import, and not hasty or crude imaginations, occurring at the impulse of the moment. True, indeed, I should rather have given them under more favorable circumstances, a more logical and philosophical form; but this is not the most popular, nor, to the great mass, the most intelligible form. At the request of some who heard them, and of many who heard of them, I am induced to publish the identical draft which I read to the audience, with only a very few verbal alterations.

I think the subject of *demons* is one that fairly comes in the path of every student of the New Testament, and ought to be well understood; and as the reader will doubtless have observed, I regard it as constituting an irrefragable proof of a spiritual system, a full refutation of that phantasm called Materialism, to those who admit the authority of Jesus Christ and the twelve Apostles. To such it is more than a mere refutation of Materialism—it is a demonstration of a separate existence of the spirits of the dead—an unequivocal evidence of a spiritual system, and of a future state of rewards and punishments.

A. C.

MORE RESTORATION MOVEMENT BOOKS FROM COBB PUBLISHING

Alexander Campbell: A Collection (Volume 2)

Abner Jones: A Collection

The Eternal Kingdom: A History of the Church of Christ

Life of Elder Walter Scott

Memoirs of Elder Thomas Campbell

Life of Raccoon John Smith

Biographical Sketches of Pioneer Preachers of Indiana

Life and Work of R.C. Barrow

Life of Knowles Shaw, Singing Evangelist

Pardee Butler: The Definitive Collection

Autobiography of Barton W. Stone

Rice Haggard: Forgotten Soldier of the Restoration

The Cane Ridge Meetinghouse: Updated Edition

Life of James O'Kelly

Recollections of Men of Faith

Early Relation and Separation of Baptists and Disciples

Origin of the Disciples of Christ

AND MANY MORE!

Available from:
Amazon.com, BarnesAndNoble.com, BooksAMillion.com, and
CobbPublishing.com